LETTER TO
ANWEI:

AN EXPLANATION OF HUMAN
IDENTITY AND
TRANSGENERATIONAL ETHICS

BY C.B. ROBERTSON

ISBN: 9781983006470

For Juniper.

With gratitude to Augustus for your criticism and encouragement,

And to Sierra, without whom none of this would have been possible.

TABLE OF CONTENTS

Identity   1

Death   7

Anwei: The Transgenerational Identity   14

Living with Anwei   25

Identity and Justice   40

The Failure of Ignorance   52

Becoming the Anwei   74

Individualism with a Home   92

Appendix A: Liberty   100

Appendix B: Peace   106

Appendix C: Christianity   112

LETTER TO ANWEI

I. IDENTITY

Dear grandchild,

I am writing this to you, rather than to my own children, because children tend not to listen to their parents. I did not listen to mine, and I have every reason to believe that you are likely not paying any heed to yours. I hope that in place of their advice and wisdom, you might listen to me, because grandparents can sometimes be a little more interesting than parents, and dead ancestors more interesting still.

What I hope to give to you is the most valuable thing that I can give. When I was younger, I tried to figure out what was most worth caring about. What matters in life? What is most worth loving?

How can you live a good life and find meaning in it?

I spent ten years caring deeply about these sorts of questions, and I studied business, power, politics, philosophy, and religion. All of these are important, but they are all transient. They do not last, and are not as satisfying as I had hoped they might be, as answers to the questions of what matters, what is worth caring about and loving, and how to live a good life.

This letter concerns what is lasting, what I believe is an answer to these questions, should they interest you. I believe it is an old answer concerning identity, one tacitly understood by generations of the distant past, but which has been forgotten in recent times. When I was growing up, we did not even have a word for it. Please grant me the patience to wind my way towards this idea with some explanation.

§

As a young adult, I assume that you have learned that the only way to accomplish anything is to invest yourself in your desired goal. Perhaps you spend time making something; perhaps you work hard to earn the money to buy an object; perhaps you take a course to learn a skill. All of these are investments of yourself in the present so that you might be better off in the future. This is how people become talented athletes, good employees, high-grade students, accomplished musicians, or anything else you might hope to become.

An old Greek philosopher named Heraclitus once said that a man can never step in the same river twice, because it is not the same river, and he is not the same man. There is some truth to this. People change over time; they cannot stay the same even if they wanted to. If you accept Heraclitus' view that we are different people from moment to moment, then you might say that the success of *future* you is dependent upon the investments of *present* you. Your practice, study, attention, and effort transform into a legacy that your future self inherits.

Of course, this may all sound a little strange. Unless you are suffering from a very rare psychological disorder, you probably feel very much like one person. You feel as if you are the same person today that you were yesterday, and will be tomorrow. Nevertheless, you probably recognize that you are not *exactly* the same today as you were yesterday.

People do change over time. If we change enough, can we truly say we are the same person?

There is an old puzzle about this question called the "Ship of Theseus" problem. Theseus was a hero from the city of Athens who slew the minotaur of the labyrinth in Crete. His ship became famous in Greek storytelling because after he set sail for home, he forgot to change the color of his sail, as he had promised his father he would if his journey had been successful. Seeing his son's ship on the horizon and seeing the black sails instead of the victorious white sails, Theseus' father Aegeus assumed that Theseus had died, and killed himself in grief. The Athenian people were so moved by the successful defeat of the ferocious minotaur and the tragic death of Aegeus that they kept and maintained Theseus's ship in the harbor for several hundred years. So everyone became familiar with Theseus' famous ship.

Over the decades and centuries that it sat in the harbor, the ship needed repairs to stay afloat. First a few planks from the sea-water, then a mast from a particularly windy and damaging storm. The ropes needed to be replaced after salt-spray and hot sun wore them away. Then one day, the sailors and shipwrights realized that after all of these years, not a single part from the original boat remained. And one worker asked the question: "is it the same ship?"

It is a surprisingly tricky question. If you say "it is the same ship because it looks the same," then I may be able to point out a dozen other boats on the Mediterranean of the same construction and appearance. They may even have been built by the same shipwright. Yet none of those are the Ship of Theseus; none of those carried the minotaur-slayer home from Crete, or flew the black sail instead of the white on that fateful journey home. It isn't just the materials, the design, or the appearance. Something about what makes the ship of Theseus *the ship of Theseus* is in its history, and in the connection between that history and the present.

But let us return to yourself. Your body is not so different from a ship. It is constantly breaking down and rebuilding itself. Your skeletal system is completely replaced every seven to ten years. Your skin is replaced every two to three weeks, and some of your internal organ components take even less time. And your brain, though composed of a stable set of neurons, is constantly changing and modifying, breaking down and strengthening pathways that form our habits and memories. That's how we learn and forget things. With all of this change going on, how can we say that you are the same person today that you were yesterday? Are you the same person? Clearly you *feel* like the same person, but are you?

That feeling of continuity matters. It is similar to that history and continuity with the past that makes the ship of Theseus unique. You feel like you are the same person because you share memories with your past self. Your decisions and actions are a part of your history, and the transition between your past self and your present self is so smooth that it feels continuous. If you think of your conscious experience as a kind of race, it feels more like a marathon than a relay race. It doesn't feel as though there are constant baton hand-offs going on. This is not to say that the stuff that you are made of is not also a part of you and your history, of course, even if your cells are constantly changing. Your body shapes your experience of the world, after all.

All of this is to say that what makes you *you* is a combination of your remembered history and the stuff that you are made of. However, I think that there is one more component. I'm sure I must sound like a bit of a Hellenophile at this point, but there is a Greek word, *telos*, meaning "end," which is used philosophically to refer to the ultimate aim or purpose of something.

A boat is built to travel across the water, so we could say the end for which it was built—its *telos*—is marine travel. Humans are made—by God, or evolution, or something else—to do what humans do. Humans, after all, are much more complex than boats. A friend of mine once joked that a sheep is a machine for converting grass into sheep, and I suppose humans are a little like that too, but if a human were to do away with hunting, farming, negotiating, marrying, working, driving, complaining, and laughing, and if he were to simply wander the fields, running from predators and eating enormous quantities of grass, we might be right to say he is more sheep or cow than man. Something about who you are lies in your purpose—your *telos*—and in the means that you might employ to achieve that end.

So you are made up of stuff, of history, and of your ultimate purpose, just as I am. These three things remain, and make us who we are, even as parts of us may change, or even die. Some people describe feeling like they have to be different people in different situations, like they have to put on a different mask in front of their coworkers, or their family, or their friends. While we all wear different masks in different circumstances, no one would say that you lose your identity every time you go to work. There is still a core underneath that remains the same. You will feel like a coherent individual, like "one" instead of "many," when the masks are in harmony with that core.

You and I share a special relationship where identity is concerned. I told you that the present "you" is inheriting the decisions and choices of the past "you," but not everything that you inherit is your own making. If the present you can inherit the decisions and choices of the past you, and if you also inherit the decisions and choices of other people, might there be some similarity between these two types of inheritance? I believe that there is, and this similarity has implications in understanding what we are and how best to live. We are getting closer to the idea I hope to convey to you, but first, allow me one more introductory digression.

II. Death

Everyone has to die one day. For the longest time, I believed that this was just the way things were for everything, a kind of law of the universe that all living things died eventually. But I learned that this was not true; some organisms seem to just keep on going. The jellyfish *Turritopsis dohmii*, for example, seems to be amortal, or "biologically immortal," meaning that it does not age in the ordinary sense. With most life, the odds of natural death increase with age, so that a 75 year old man is more likely to die than a 65 year old man. This is not the case with biologically immortal things. For them, it is a dice-roll with the same dice every time. A lucky *dohmii* might wind up living a thousand years, whereas no human, no matter how fortunate, is going to make it much past 120.

And jellyfish aren't the only ones. Planarian worms (class *Turbellaria*), the Rougheye Rockfish (*Sebastes aleutianus*), the Olm (*Proteus anguinus*), several species of turtles (*Chrysemys picta, Emydoidea blandingii, Terrapene carolina*), the Red Sea Urchin (*Strongylocentrotus franciscanus*), the Ocean Quahog Clam (*Arctica islandica*), the Greenland Shark (*Somniosus microcephalus*), and the Great Basin Bristlecone Pine (*Pinus longaeva*), all do not age. If left to themselves, they do not die.

What allows these particular creatures to live without dying? If you look at their environments, the answer becomes apparent. All of these immortal things live in stasis. Their environment is stable and virtually unchanging. The sea-creatures live in the depths of the ocean, surrounded by nothingness and other creatures that have not changed in millions of years. The 4,000 year old bristlecone pines live in arid, rocky places where it rarely even rains or snows. The only animals they'll see are the ravens, the ground-squirrels, the coyotes, and sometimes a great California Condor.

I'm sure you have been taught that all successful species fit into a niche in their ecosystem. They are adapted to their environment, and this adaptation is achieved by gradual change over time, across generations. If a species stays the same while its environment changes, it will die. If the environment does not change, however, then evolution is unnecessary. And if evolution is unnecessary, then death is unnecessary.

The implications of this were a little startling to me. It would seem that immortality is biologically possible in some cases. But what about humans? For us, immortality is evolutionarily undesirable.

To understand how this could be, consider your brain. You were born with more neural connections than you will have at any other point in your life, because learning isn't mostly about making connections. It's about *pruning* them. We can never get back the neurons we lose, and it is harder to build new connections than it is to cut them. By the time you are 25 or 26 years old, your world-view will be more or less set. You will be able to learn new things, but you will probably have a hard time adapting if something fundamental changed. For example, if it was conclusively demonstrated that drinking coffee was as bad for you as smoking cigarettes, I would probably have a much harder time relinquishing my morning cup than you would. If it was shown that some good organization that I had supported in my youth had recently turned evil, it would be emotionally more difficult for me to come to terms with it than it would be for you. We layer our beliefs on top of other beliefs, and after decades of this kind of stacking, the overturning of one bedrock conviction can tumble our whole worldview. Most people cannot handle such a dramatic change.

That we even live past our thirties is a testament to our adaptability. Of all the animals in the world, we humans live in the most volatile and dynamic environment of all, precisely because we are surrounded by other humans. Our own adaptability and the complexity of our environment are one and the same, and we are remarkably adaptive! But this adaptability has its limits. The older we get, the more likely we are to be left behind by our environment— the more likely we are to die. The more *necessary* it becomes that we die. If humans did not die, then we could not evolve and adapt to our changing environment. If we did not die, we would require a world that did not change.

There is one particular story I am reminded of from Lewis Carroll's *Through the Looking Glass* where the Red Queen is leading Alice on a blindingly fast run. After sprinting faster than Alice thought possible for at least ten minutes, they took a rest, only for Alice to realize that they hadn't moved anywhere at all. After Alice comments on this, the Red Queen says that here, "it takes all the running you can do to keep in the same place." I think aging is a lot like that; you have to run faster and faster to stay in the place and not get left behind. And then at some point, we can no longer keep up. It seems, then, that we were built to die; it is the culminating and final procedure of our design. Cancer, heart-disease, Alzheimer's, all of these sometimes feel as if they come too soon, but in the end, they are a natural by-product of our body's metabolic processes. They are supposed to happen. We are like fireworks, designed to shoot only so high into the air before self-destruction.

Sometimes, people take death into their own hands by committing suicide. When I was around 14 or 15 years old, some friends and I would occasionally listen to a band called *Linkin Park*. They were an enormously successful band at the time, led by a talented singer named Chester Bennington. Bennington had everything: a beautiful wife, children, fame and fortune beyond the hopes of nearly everyone who has ever lived. Then on July 20, 2017, he killed himself. He was found by a cleaning lady, hanging in the bedroom of his spectacular home in Palos Verdes Estates, California.

People today usually say that suicide is the result of depression and despair, and that depression and despair come from material failings or from not being loved. But Bennington is only one of many powerful, famous, and loved people who have killed themselves. Accompanying Bennington in 2017 was fellow musician Chris Cornell, who killed himself only a week before Bennington—also by hanging. Bennington even sang "Hallelujah" at Cornell's funeral. These two are accompanied by dozens of other sports stars, actors, musicians, and celebrities who have killed themselves in the past decade, and he will surely not be the last.

It may be tempting to believe that suicide among the powerful is a modern problem, but this turns out to be wrong. In the Theseus story, Aegeus killed himself, after all. Before even the 2nd century A.D., Hannibal, Brutus, Mark Antony, Nero, Otho, Cleopatra, Demosthenes, Cato the Younger, Metellus Scipio, and Qu Yuan all died by their own hand. Judas Iscariot hung himself before Jesus' trial in front of Pontius Pilate. And Boudica, the Celtic warrior queen, poisoned herself.

Other ancient texts referencing suicide include Plato's *Phaedo*, the Bible, Augustine's *City of God*, and Aristotle's *Nicomachean Ethics*. I have even heard it argued that Socrates' death was a suicide, because he had the chance to escape his fate but voluntarily chose to stay and drink the poison Hemlock.

Natural death may appear as an unavoidable part of nature, but suicide is harder to explain. The philosopher Albert Camus once said that there is only one truly serious philosophical problem: whether or not we should kill ourselves. But if we are the products of evolution, and if evolution is about survival and reproduction, then this question should strike you as rather strange. How is suicide a question at all? How did evolution *allow* the suicidal impulse to survive? It does not appear to be conceivably beneficial to the individual. As with other varieties of death, there is no "you" left to reap the rewards of whatever benefits suicide may bring. Who could death benefit? What purpose could suicide serve?

A friend of mine wrote an essay about the psychology of suicide[1] after Chester Bennington died

---

[1] Cassiel, Aedhan. "Chester Bennington & White Male Suicide." *Counter-Currents*, 21 July 2017, www.counter-currents.com/2017/07/chester-bennington-and-white-male-suicide/.

which sheds some light on this subject. According to his research, there are situations in which suicide makes evolutionary sense:

> *A basic sentiment commonly expressed by the suicidal is: "Everyone would be better off without me!" Evolutionary analysis suggests that suicide exists because we really do have innate mechanisms crafted to evaluate whether or not everyone would be better off without us. Why? Because if our handicaps require assistance that limits our close kin's ability to survive and reproduce, we may in fact increase our own genetic fitness more by committing suicide and removing the reproduction-limiting obligations we impose upon them than we would be going on living with the help of our kin.*

In other words, the idea of killing oneself doesn't come from not having things, but from not providing things; from not being needed, rather than not being loved. If biological success was about the individual alone, suicide would be unthinkable. Yet here it is.

Now let me be clear that in almost every instance, suicide is the wrong decision. There are very few cases where suicide is a rational choice, and fewer still for people under 40. Young people like you are the most valuable, evolutionarily speaking, because you still have all of your reproductive capabilities. I am somewhat less valuable than you are, as you will be less valuable than your grandchildren. I don't bring up the dark subject of suicide to defend the practice, but to explore what we are as humans. I hope that my explanation of where our identity comes from which follows will give you fortitude and courage to dismiss suicidal impulses should they one day come to you.

With that cleared up, we can return to our subject. Despite their vast difference in appearance, suicide and natural death actually have the same cause: it is beneficial! But who benefits from our death? To answer this question, a biologist might say that death is beneficial for "the gene." This is a good start, but I am not so sure it is a complete answer. It is like talking about a person just as "stuff," without history or *telos*. Without these other components, our stuff is just transient matter, and even our genes will change over time if these other elements are not considered.

I think there is an entity, a kind of *person*, who benefits from our life and from our death, and whose existence explains the phenomenon of suicide, and this brings me (finally) to the idea that I have wanted to convey to you.

III. Anwei: The Transgenerational Identity

Now I will describe to you this idea I have been alluding to over the last several pages.

We are partially made of history, partially made of stuff, and partially made of purpose. Think about where this stuff and purpose comes from. You didn't make your history, you inherited it, of course. But you didn't make your own stuff either. Your stuff is designed by genes, which you and I both inherited from our ancestors, who inherited it from their ancestors, and so on. And what about your *telos*? Your purpose—to follow the "human" strategies for biological success—*that* is certainly not something you or I came up with! Even your *telos* is something inherited.

I have already described to you the importance of leaving an inheritance from past you for future you. Psychologists usually describe this as "deferred gratification," and it is widely held to be one of the greatest predictors of success we have. But this principle of leaving and receiving an inheritance doesn't only apply to the individual; it applies across generations as well. The Greeks had a proverb: *a society grows great when old men plant trees whose shade they know they shall never sit in.* Your history, your *telos*, even your very body and its blueprint, all of these are a legacy you have inherited, just as I inherited mine.

We are both part of a continuous line of individuals. Just as we can think of our bodies as ships that need maintenance and repair, which remain the same ship despite planks, ropes, masts, and sails being changed—despite even the whole boat gradually being replaced!—in this same way, we are individual planks on a greater ship. You and I are both replacements for old boards, to be replaced by newer, fresher wood once we become old and rotten.

This is the great idea, the great concept. The great, eternal ship that you and I both are parts of as components, this is the old and important idea for which I could not find a name.

When I was first writing this letter to you, I called it the "transgenerational identity," as it seemed to me the most descriptively accurate label. But this eventually sounded too cumbersome. In looking for an appropriate word for this entity, I decided to borrow from Proto Indo-European roots, since the Latin and Greek ones created words just as long as "transgenerational identity." It is called "Anwei" (pronounced æn-wei[2]) from Proto-Indo-European "ane" and "wei." "Ane" means "breath" or "wind," but subsequently took on the meaning "spirit" or "soul." It is the source of words like "animate" and "animal." And "wei" simply meant "we" or "us." So the Anwei is, literally, the "spirit of us."

The animating 'we.'

The Anwei is the transcendent being that we both come from. It is the source of our inheritance, and the being for whom we leave an inheritance when we build a legacy for our children. I am speaking of "our"

---

[2] Not to be confused with "ennui," which carries almost the opposite meaning. If pronounced as "æn-wei" instead of the French "on-wee," we can avoid unnecessary confusion.

now because, as relatives, you and I are different parts of the same Anwei.

The Hindus believe that Gods would sometimes come to earth in human forms. These humans were "avatars" of the Gods, usually immensely powerful, and possessing some—but not all—of the deity's qualities. That is what you are. You are an avatar of our Anwei, this aggregation of legacy in history, form, and *telos* that made us who we are, and makes our investment in our descendants something worthwhile, and not just arbitrary altruism. It is our genes, it is our lineage, it is our history, our culture, our language, our nature, and our collective inheritance.

It is what compelled me to write this letter to you.

We cannot live forever like a jellyfish, bristlecone pine, or sea turtle. You and I will both die. But our Anwei can live forever. It is amortal, and through it, you and I can be a part of something that lives forever.

§

I understand that this idea of the Anwei may sound a little bit far-fetched to you, maybe even a little superstitious. It is up to you whether you anthropomorphize this concept as I do, or think of it merely as an abstract concept, like one of Plato's forms[3]. I don't think anything is lost in either case.

---

[3] Plato believed that the reality was more accurately understood to be comprised of ideas, or "forms," rather than comprised of objects. He believed that the forms came first, and that the objects proceed from the forms. In this system, you could consider a particular chair to be, in a sense, less real than the idea of "chair."

But if you are like me, you may see three problem with this theory: first, isn't this very similar to othe concepts, like race and ethnicity? Second, you do not *feel* like this Anwei, and if you do not feel like something, how can it be a part of your identity? Third, what are the boundaries of the Anwei? Doesn't the haziness around the edges of this concept make it somewhat arbitrary, and perhaps even made up? For simplicity's sake, I will call these the "race question," "phenomenology[4] problem," and the "border problem."

The Race Question

The Anwei is not the same as race or ethnicity, although it is related to these concepts, and is very close to the idea of lineage. A race is a geographically identifiable and genetically distinct population, while an ethnicity is a broader cultural identity, often associated with a particular race. These are descriptive terms for someone looking from the outside in, and it is entirely possible to be of the same race and ethnicity as someone else, but not to share the same unifying Anwei. The Anwei is narrower than either race or ethnicity, and is closer to a Scottish Clan or an Israeli Tribe than to something as vast and experientially abstract as an entire race. Multiple clans can make up a racial nation (the Scots), and an entire nation may be descended from a single ancestor (the Jews), but in both cases, it does not make sense to think of the entire nation as "one

---

[4] "Phenomenology" is the study of our conscious experience of things, rather than the study of things as themselves.

tribe." Each is broken up: into roughly three hundred in the case of the Scots, and into twelve in the case of the Jews. These smaller clans or tribes are something concrete, closer to the populations of primordial human societies that we evolved to feel comfortable within and to connect with[5]. It is in these smaller groups that we can actually connect with others in a meaningful manner.

Is the Anwei just a clan or a tribe then?

Not quite. The clan or tribe is a legal or quasi-legal organization, sort of like a nation or a soccer team. The establishment of a recognized "clan" or "tribe" identity is an accomplishment and an aid to the Anwei, but the Anwei exists prior to such an official establishment, and can exist with or without such recognition. It is the groundwork beneath the clan or tribe. The Anwei can die while the "tribe" lives on in name and appearance, but to those who knew it before, it will feel like a hollow and empty association compared to its former self.

The Phenomenology Problem

The phenomenology problem is that you do not experience yourself as a part of this Anwei, but as yourself, an individual. I believe this can be answered by exploring the nature of consciousness.

To begin with, look closely at your feeling of self. Try paying attention to this experience of self-ness. Can you find it? Is it located somewhere in your chest? In your head?

---

[5] See "Dunbar's number."

If you look carefully, you will notice that the self cannot be located anywhere. "You" vanish when you try to find the center of your experience, of your self.

This is because the feeling of being you does not have one source, but many. You may intuitively imagine that your feeling of self is located somewhere inside your skull because that is where your eyes are, and your conscious experience of the world is heavily dominated by vision. But if you were to close your eyes and try to navigate in a dark room by touch, the boundaries of you would expand from your skull to your hands and feet. If you used a feeling rod like a blind person and grew acclimated enough to using it, you might even feel as though the rod were a part of you, that it was *you* touching the coffee table or chair leg, rather than the rod.

What you consciously experience is the result of what you pay attention to, and your attention is highly malleable. You are perfectly capable of paying prolonged and intense attention to high literature while completely neglecting the world of science, and equally capable of the inverse. Your experience of who you are and what you are is highly dependent upon the allocation of your attention, and your attention can be divided into infinite variations or concentrations. So while your consciousness may have something to do with your identity, the fact that you are not here and now experiencing yourself as a part of the Anwei is not evidence of its absence, just as an orphan may still be the offspring of their biological parents, despite never knowing them directly.

I am not trying to tell you that "you" don't exist because you cannot find your center. In fact, it is exactly that kind of reasoning that prevents people from being able to connect with the Anwei: "we cannot find it, so it does not exist." You cannot find the center of an ant colony either.

Sure, the Queen may be the literal 'center,' but there is no reason to believe that the Queen is the "essence" of the colony. Since workers and make up the overwhelming majority of the population of the colony, if we were to imagine what it is "like" to be an ant colony, the experience of the workers might be a closer approximation than the experience of the queen.

But this is just daydreaming. The fact is that you exist in the way that an ant colony exists. No ant knows what it feels like to be a colony, just as no skin cell or lone neuron knows what it is like to be you. The Anwei can exist, and you can be a part of the Anwei, without feeling as if you were its manifestation.

All of this is to say that your sense of "self" is remarkably malleable and decentralized. Consciousness is a fascinating and complicated subject, one which I am perhaps underqualified to describe to you in any more detail, but it should be clear to you that your "true self" is not necessarily revealed by how you feel. People sometimes feel depressed, drunk, ecstatic, bored, cheery, or awe-inspired; sometimes, we are asleep and feel nothing at all! None of these feelings—or lack thereof—say very much about *what* you are, just as the feelings (or lack thereof) of an ant say very little about what it is. The fact that you do not feel like a part of the Anwei does not mean that you are not a part of it. Later, I will show you that it is actually possible to develop a closer experiential connection to the Anwei.

The Boundary Problem

That leaves us with the boundary problem: where are the edges of the Anwei? Doesn't the haziness around the edges of this concept make it somewhat arbitrary, and perhaps even made up? For example, if two people from different lineages have a child, which Anwei is it a part of? If we cannot find these borders, if they are constantly mixing and evolving, does the Anwei even exist?

This may sound strange after discussing the geographic mystery of consciousness, where a lack of boundaries is not proof of nonexistence, but this is subtly different. With consciousness, there is at least a conceptual boundary; it does not extend beyond our attention.

My claim is that the Anwei is not only a concept, but a kind of living being, in the manner of an ant colony. The colony is greater than the ants which make it up, and can survive even if every ant presently within it eventually dies off. But the colony still has boundaries: the insects—even ants—outside of the *system* comprising the colony are not a part of the colony. The geography outside of the nest itself isn't considered a part of the colony. Even an individual ant *from the colony*, by itself, is not the colony.

All living things have boundaries that differentiate the organism from the outside world. Animals have a skin which makes this division intuitive and obvious, but larger, older, and more complicated organisms, or even concepts, are sometimes more difficult to pin down.

Consider the case of Pando[6], or "the Trembling Giant." Pando appears to be thousands of individual Quaking Aspen trees (*Populus tremuloides*) spread over 100 acres near Fish Lake, Utah, each individually appearing only 20-30 years old, perhaps 50 or 60 in some case. In reality, all of these trees are genetically identical, and share a living root structure that is at least 80,000 years old, and may in fact be a million years old or more[7]. It is what is known as a "clonal colony" organism. Clonal colonies have a genetic source and reproduce by spreading, rather than through sexual reproduction. The Aspen is not the only organism that does this; just to stay within plants, Devil's Club, Hazelnut, Sumac, and the Creosote bush also sometimes form clonal colonies.

What makes Pando and these other cloning organisms interesting is that the boundaries of the living thing in question are ambiguous. Is Pando one organism or tens of thousands? By appearances, it certainly looks like thousands. Only by examining the nature and essence of *identity*—of what it means for a thing to be itself—can we see that these "individual" trees are in fact one being, however difficult it may be to identify their boundaries.

Other things can have ambiguous edges, yet we have no difficulty differentiating them from the outside world. Something as simple as a river can

---

[6] Latin for "I spread."

[7] Grant, Michael. "The Trembling Giant." *Discover*, 1 Oct, 1993.
http://discovermagazine.com/1993/oct/thetremblinggian
285.

have boundaries that fluctuate with the seasons or the weather, looking dramatically different in a winter flood than during a summer drought. I'm reminded of Heraclitus' quote again: is it the same river? Clearly it is. The variation is a part of its nature.

But!—you may object—what about a river like the Colorado? Over thousands of years, it has cut away at the rock and worn a new path for itself. It will never look like it did before. Is the Colorado the same river as it was 10,000 years ago?

Perhaps. Perhaps not. What I do know is that the old river is a part of the history of the present, and that they share a source in the Rocky Mountains and a destination in the Gulf of California. Like a person, the river changes in form as it ages and fulfills its destiny (its predetermined natural course), but no one would say that a boy has transformed into a different person because he has become a man. The Colorado of today is the same river as the Colorado of 10,000 years ago, even if it may have looked dramatically different then. By contrast, the Colorado is not the same river as the Columbia, despite looking somewhat similar in a few places. They have different sources, different forms, and different destinations. They are both rivers, but have completely and wholly different identities.

Variation is required within evolution, and within every organizational level of human life, but that does not eliminate the possibility of a shared identity. Identity defines the general constraints within which variation is allowed, and sets the standard for which variations actually *improve* the quality of the thing in question. Having a shared identity doesn't mean that a group of things lack variety; it means that there are broad patterns of commonality in history, nature, and purpose, which make the variations meaningful.

In this way, the ambiguities in identifying where a particular Anwei might begin, merge, or end do not disprove the concept. You and I are very different from each other, in our genes and in our background, but we still both come from a common history not shared by the rest of humanity, and we share combinations of traits that are unique to us. Neither of us will have *all* of the traits that describe this animating 'we.' No one does. The Colorado River will never be the river that everyone remembers it as, because the river is always changing, and people's memories stay the same. But it is the same river, and you and are a part of the same Anwei, even if it is not exactly the same as it was 10,000 years ago.

IV. Living with Anwei

Dear grandchild, if the culture you have been born into is anything like mine, then this conception of what we truly are will be profound, maybe even shocking. All through my early years, I was variously taught by much of the culture that I was entirely an individual, unique and unlike anyone else. I was taught that I should develop myself *for myself*, as an individual. If I did this, then I would be happy and successful. This modern wisdom sounds intuitive, but I believe it actually sets young people out on the wrong foot, and can even make you unhappy and unsuccessful. I hope to show you that those who live in alignment with their Anwei not only live happier, more meaningful, and more successful lives; they actually live *longer* too. Later on, I will explain how the Anwei can lead you toward becoming a true individual, but that is something to graduate to. I am getting ahead of myself.

My parents subscribed to *National Geographic* magazine, and when I was younger, I would browse through them, reading articles as research for school papers, or sometimes just for fun. But one of the articles that stuck out to me the longest when I read it was called "The Secrets of Long Life[8]." The subjects of the article were three different communities: one in Sardinia, Italy, one in Okinawa, Japan, and one in Loma Linda, California. All three of these communities saw their older members regularly

---

[8] Buettner, Dan. "The Secrets of Long Life." *National Geographic*, Nov 2005. https://www.bluezones.com/wp-content/uploads/2015/01/Nat_Geo_LongevityF.pdf.

living into their 80's, 90's, even into their 100's, at extraordinary rates.

Now most explanations for longevity begin with individual health-choices—refraining from smoking, limiting sugar, getting enough exercise, and so on. Some scientists pay attention to the genetic influences that give some people a leg-up in living longer. These things certainly matter, and the author noted that all three of these communities ate relatively healthy diets, stayed active, and benefited from good genetics which predisposed them toward reaching very old age. But these communities are matched by populations nearby with similar genetics, similar diet, and comparable degrees of exercise, whose occupants still do not live as long. The extra ingredient, it seems, is connection with other people, especially family.

The Sardinians would be up early in the morning, milking cows, slaughtering sheep, raising pigs, or chopping wood—whatever needed to be done around the farm. But for lunch or dinner, they would all sit together for meals with their extended family. They lived in an "honor culture," where you are considered to be responsible for (and to) your group, not merely yourself. While this responsibility can be demanding, it also gives its members something meaningful to do with their time. I'm sure you can see the connection here with the Anwei.

The Okinawans also enjoyed the benefits of a healthy diet and active lifestyle, working hard like the Sardinians all the way into their 80's and 90's. In Okinawa, they have a word, *ikigai* (生き甲斐), which translates roughly as your "reason for being," or your "reason for getting out of bed in the morning." Most

Okinawans describe their *ikigai* as their friends and family, or the role that they play within the community, be it a fisher or a gardener. It is a socially-derived feeling of purpose (*telos*) that drives these people to live longer and happier lives. I remember that there was one woman in the article who was 103 years old, and her daughter said that her longevity brought pride to the whole family and village. That's a kind of honor culture, very similar to the Sardinians.

The community featured in Loma Linda, California was a group of Seventh-Day Adventists, a variety of Protestant Christians that celebrate Saturday as the holy day of rest, rather than Sunday. The author noted that regular religious attendance and participation is known to increase lifespan by as much as two years, but subsequent research has revealed that he may have been understating the case by at least three years[9]. For these Seventh-Day Adventists, rejecting alcohol, cigarettes, and pork were all biblical injunctions, not merely health ones, and aside from the explicitly banned foods, they had fostered a culture that discouraged caffeinated beverages, rich, sugary foods, or anything too "stimulating."

But as important as their health habits are, their culture of socializing and helping others seemed to separate them more profoundly from the broad variety of other health-cultures in the United States in terms of longevity. One woman, at 101 years old,

[9] Wallace, Laura et all. "Does Religion Stave Off the Grave?" *Social Psychological and Personality Science*, 13 June 2018. http://journals.sagepub.com/doi/10.1177/1948550618779820.

would wake up in the morning and work out before going to assist at an elderly day-care center, often helping people two or three decades younger than herself. Like staying healthy, the Adventists viewed helping others as a religious obligation, and as a result, they lived in an insular, family and community-oriented society of like-minded people.

Just like the Sardinians and the Okinawans.

All three of these groups live in close alignment with their Anwei. None of these individuals live *as* individuals, but live as Sardinians, as Okinawans, as Seventh-Day Adventists. They are reflections of their groups, accepting the legacy offered to them, and building upon it for those who are to come after them. They are *one with their people*, living in spiritual conformity with their group, and this brings them longevity, prosperity, and happiness.

But the best information we have on longevity, identity, and happiness isn't from *National Geographic*. It comes from the Harvard Study of Adult Development[10], which tracked the lives of 724 men over more than 75 years. What the researchers found was that having relationships is perhaps the single most important factor in living a long and happy life:

We've learned three big lessons about relationships. The first is that social connections are really good for us, and that loneliness kills. It

[10] Waldinger, Robert. "What makes a good life? Lessons from the longest study on happiness." *TEDx*, Nov 2015. https://www.ted.com/talks/robert_waldinger_what_make s_a_good_life_lessons_from_the_longest_study_on_happi ness

turns out that people who are more socially connected to family, to friends, to community, are happier, they're physically healthier, and they live longer than people who are less well connected. And the experience of loneliness turns out to be toxic. People who are more isolated than they want to be from others find that they are less happy, their health declines earlier in midlife, their brain functioning declines sooner and they live shorter lives than people who are not lonely. And the sad fact is that at any given time, more than one in five Americans will report that they're lonely.

And we know that you can be lonely in a crowd and you can be lonely in a marriage, so the second big lesson that we learned is that it's not just the number of friends you have, and it's not whether or not you're in a committed relationship, but it's the quality of your close relationships that matters. It turns out that living in the midst of conflict is really bad for our health. High-conflict marriages, for example, without much affection, turn out to be very bad for our health, perhaps worse than getting divorced. And living in the midst of good, warm relationships is protective.[11]

I'm sure to many younger people like yourself, this may sound like boring and stodgy traditionalism. But I think the appeal is more universal. One of my favorite musicians from my early twenties was an

---

[11] The third lesson is that social connectedness staves off cognitive decline (Alzheimer's, etc.); loneliness, in other words, is bad for your brain.

outspoken political progressive named Maynard James Keenan, who wrote and sang for bands like *Tool*, *A Perfect Circle*, and *Puscifer*. You may not know of these bands, but they were remarkably successful in their time, especially *Tool*.

But it is not Keenan's musical success that is of interest here. Keenan was also a wine-maker, owning Merkin Vineyards and Caduceus Cellars in Jerome, Arizona. Because I do not wish to speak for Keenan, and in any case cannot phrase his ideology any more perfectly than he does for himself, I have included a few quotes from a short documentary[12] about hiFs wine-making operations and his world-view that informs it. These quotes are a little long, but I hope you will read them, as they are valuable and enjoyable to hear, especially coming from a musical celebrity:

> *What I'm doing out here in Arizona—there's this word "sustainable" that we throw around that I feel is applicable. Not just in terms of a small economy, or a larger global economy, all those things, I think that it also applies just to an artist and their creative flow. You see a lot of guys who are successful earlier on, and they start to not be successful and they get a little desperate. Desperate to be relevant in a world that no longer understands them.*

When I heard Keenan say this, I was reminded of the older people who did not, or could not, run fast enough and who were left behind by society. Lone

---

[12] Shinn, Travis, director. "The Art of Work with Maynard James Keenan." *Revolver*, 17 Apr. 2017. www.youtube.com/watch?v=hrcJz63n94.

individuals have a hard time with continuing the run, and it is a constant struggle to stay relevant. As my friend Aedhan said, relevance is important in finding the will to keep going. Being needed by others is something we need ourselves, and that need is hard to find if we are untethered individuals, floating between places and people without a transcendent center.

We have a lot of disconnect. We have plenty of food, plenty of clothing, plenty of shelter at this point. Now we're just kind of wrath, eating each other and eating ourselves. We've lost touch with that friction, that friction that keeps you moving, keeps you on your toes, keeps you growing. Keeps you learning. Keeps you surviving. We've kind of lost touch with that, in a way. We've lost touch with that creative side, I think. Our utilitarian side.

This is an attempt to rekindle some of that. To understand how vulnerable we actually are. How much we are not actually in charge. And to keep that art alive, keep those stories alive. I have much more to say now, in music, in words, with this endeavor.

Your inheritance is not just what your ancestors leave for you. Part of it is nature itself. Part of it is the struggle both with and against nature that your ancestors undertook as a matter of survival, and the further you separate yourself from the struggles that characterized the stories of Job and Odysseus, of Ernest Hemingway and Jack London—of your own ancestors—the further you get from all that, the less relevant their underlying spirit will be to you. I think if you get too far away from nature, you become less human.

> *I do what I do because I enjoy it. I enjoy farming, I enjoy wine-making, I enjoy writing music, I enjoy performing songs, writing songs, just in general doing. And I'm always going to be doing. Whether I'm relevant or not I think is irrelevant, because I'm going to do what I'm going to do regardless of whether somebody knows about it or not. It's just in my nature. So you can see in the studio, I'm always writing, I'm always working with Tool, A Perfect Circle, Puscifer, all the time. Just slowly hedging our way through it all to present. If I was just doing those things, you start to run out of actual life experiences. All you're going to write about is the bus, or a [...] lawsuit. You're going to lose your way, become disconnected. This [the vineyard] is the reconnect.*

Other people are the building block of legacy, but connecting with the Anwei isn't the same as connecting with just anyone. Sometimes connecting with the Anwei means ignoring those who happen to be nearby—perhaps those in your school, or at work, or fellow artists in the music world. In principle, the connection with the Anwei doesn't even require other living people. What feels natural to you? What is your true nature? These are challenging questions to answer because we are so heavily influenced by our environment in our early years. It can be hard to distinguish between what is from the Anwei and what is from the rest of the world—this being the prerequisite understanding so that you will be able to differentiate what is *beneficial* to the Anwei, which may include some outside influence, and what is detrimental to it. But over time, you may be able to discover the Anwei in yourself, without other people. This is a difficult skill to develop, but it can be of great value. If the people you are surrounded by are people in your occupation or role, then your life will reflect only what is meaningful to that occupation or role. If you are a musician, this might mean the tour-bus and lawsuits, at least according to Keenan. But no matter how the values of these roles and occupations look, they will lead you away from what is most important. They will lead you away from the Anwei.

It is better to be surrounded by others you can grow and learn from. But in cases where those around you are on a different path, it is better to trust yourself and your own instincts.

As a legacy, I feel like some of the music we've done will live on its own. But I feel like... using [David] Bowie as an example. Bowie passes away. People line up to freak out that he's gone, and they're reverent about what he's done, and in a way, that's done. He's done it, he can't do any more, he's no longer here. So there's a reverence to him, and a worship of sorts; a fan reaction to what he has done, and now he is no longer here. But that's kind of one direction.

What we've done, what we're setting up as a community here in northern Arizona [...] with the wine-making and just the culinary efforts, and the community efforts that go along with it and all the collateral benefits of a wine-making and grape-

growing community, there might be some founders of that movement.

But if we are no longer here, there are other people that continue what we've started. So in a way, that's more of a legacy because you've actually established something that can continue a hundred, two hundred years beyond you, which sets up that artistic process: wine-making, food-growing, all the industries that surround that, all the activities that surround it, and of course, the art of celebrating those struggles, because as a wine-maker, you need grapes. So you are a slave to the sun and the rain. You are a slave to mother nature, to understand her processes and what she wants, and she does not care what you want. You're having to work around that. So that celebration around the fire, at the end of a long hunt of a long agricultural endeavor, that art, that's what tells the story of what struggles you've gone through. It's the celebration of life, along with the struggle of actually trying to survive.

Keenan may be a little unfair to Bowie here. Rock music is a tradition, with regional epicenters in Los Angeles, London, New York, Seattle, Nashville, and elsewhere, and musicians become inspired and influenced by other musicians in an organic fashion, just like chefs, painters, architects, and other artists. But he is right to say that a real legacy is not a one-way street. It is a dialogue across time which can grow and adapt. A real legacy is not a statue, but a living thing.

On the subject of life, Christian theologians would distinguish between two different kinds of life:

bios (βίος), and *zoe* (ζωή). *Bios* refers to physical life and the material it is comprised of (it is the etymological root of "biology"). *Zoe* refers to the life of the spirit, and in its nature and effects, it is similar to *ikigai*. What Keenan's talk of reconnection and art conveys is that finding the Anwei is not just the source of *bios* life; it is a deep well of *zoe* life as well.

> *If you really kind of look at it, your legacy, if executed properly in the nuances that I identify with it, it's not so much about you. It's about laying groundwork and honoring your past, and honoring your family, and going forward for your children and their children. And you're setting up a foundation where they still have to struggle. Just laying it out for them and just handing them a big bank account, that's not going to help them. They have to struggle in some way, they have to earn this thing. I feel like vineyards, wineries, and the music, is something that requires some struggle. You have to find your way in it, you can't just be handed it.*

I believe that stories are the greatest inheritance that you can leave for your descendants, so the best thing we can do is to live a great story. Great stories are like magic: they appear impossible, and inspire hope, awe, and courage in those who see or hear about them. Stories are the substance of the Anwei.

There is no story in inheriting a lot of money. Often times—especially in modern times—there is not even much of a story in making a lot of money. I know that wealth can be very helpful for individuals, like you and me. But it's not about us. To the Anwei, wealth is an interesting byproduct, perhaps an indicator of good things, but of no consequence on its own. Be careful not to overemphasize the value of money to your children. As I have said, true legacies are living things, and money is a dead thing. Leaving your children an enormous financial inheritance is more often a curse than a blessing.

Keenan's legacy is not just stories. He has woven an elaborate tapestry of interlocking habits, rituals, and relationships, with his musicians, his growers, his cooks, his customers, his family, even with the land itself. Each of these habits and rituals and relationships—from the seasonal planting and harvesting rituals to the presentation and tasting of wine to the picking out of a melody on a guitar—all of these are things that Keenan's great-grandchildren can participate in. Through their own participation, they can connect with Keenan himself. If they do so, then Keenan will have already found his connection with them, the unborn.

This is living in connection with the Anwei.

The Verde Valley in general, it's not for everybody. This area of Arizona, it's one of those things. You have to resonate with this area to really dig in and be here. It'll spit you out like a bad liver transplant.

There is pride and self-respect in being able to live and thrive in a selective environment. Stories and legacies come from "friction," and living in a safe, easy world without this friction will limit your ability to write a meaningful story or leave a living legacy.

36

But there is a deeper importance in the land than merely the selectivity that leads to pride:

> *Speaking form an artist's perspective, there's various kinds of canvas, but canvas is canvas, paints are kind of paints... look that guy's a painter, and that guy's a painter, I'll just get one of the paintings, right? They're going to be the same, because it's just paint and canvas and a guy painting. Well that's not the case, obviously. Wine kind of takes that to another level because it's expressing a place. Every single place is going to express a particular variety differently. If you have Cabernet Sauvignon on this site, as opposed to Napa or Texas or New Mexico or Washington State, Oregon, they're all going to be different expressions of that grape because there is an infinite number of variables.*
>
> *This [land] is a huge copper mine. A little volcanic activity here, it used to be the bottom of the ocean, so there's limestone, caliche layers, decomposed granite, river sediment from all the creeks and rivers. You're near the Grand Canyon, we're at high elevation, so that diurnal swing, night to day, is going to be different than it would be in Napa. All these variables go into making that grape a unique thing on that site, and then that lifetime of trying to figure out what grapes do best in that region. Since we have no actual history or notes from here, we won't know the answer to that question for another fifty years.*

I will tell you more about the importance of land shortly. But I think the most important summarizing

37

words from Maynard James Keenan on the subject of the Anwei come from his website. In his bio excerpt from Caduceus Cellars, he had this to say:

> *Having already dove headfirst into this venture, I found out from a distant relative that wine making is in my blood. My Great Grandfather, "Spirito" Marzo, had vineyards and made wine in Venaus, Italy, just North of Turino in Piemonte. My tastes in wine reflect this history. It's even apparent in my choice of home. Clearly I and my fathers are one.*

"I and my fathers are one."
Nothing more perfectly captures the idea of the Anwei than that.

§

I hope you can see now that it is possible to live in harmony with this spirit, because people have done it. We may not be able to see or touch a culture; we cannot feel a nation; we cannot taste or smell "history." You cannot point to an ant colony, or to a river, in their completion. Yet all of these things exist as concepts and patterns with explanatory value. It is in this manner that we can know that your Anwei exists. The fact that we die, and sometimes even willingly kill ourselves, is evidence that it exists. That we would willingly die for another person has confused evolutionary psychologists and biologists for decades, but it is no mystery that we should be willing to die for a greater whole, of which we are only a part. It is a whole that is responsible for our existence, and which grants us continued life of a kind after our death. The Anwei is as much "you" as you are the Anwei, after all.

But more importantly, it should be clear that it is better to live in this way, in accordance with your true identity with the Anwei. It brings more happiness, purpose, and life than trying to live for yourself, on your own. You are a social animal, belonging to a pack like wolves, lions, or chimpanzees. It is part of your nature to be an integrated part of this group, and what animal can be happy living against itself?

V. Identity and Justice

Dear grandchild, so far, I have described to you how this concept of the Anwei makes greater sense of the idea of human life, as well as how it improves the duration and experience of life. But I believe there is one more area in which the truth and importance of the Anwei can be demonstrated. That is the realm of morality and justice. Without the Anwei, and looking through the lens of the independent individual, the subject of justice presents a paradox that underlies a great deal of unnecessary political and social disagreement. I believe that remembering the Anwei can resolve this disagreement, and make better sense of human experience and political society as we see it.

Let me begin by introducing this paradox to you. Imagine that you are observing two rooms. Each room contains a button on the wall and a table in the middle. The button will dispense money when pressed, but it is sealed behind a sheet of glass, and the only way to slide back the glass and uncover the button is to solve a puzzle located on the table. The trouble is that puzzle is extremely difficult. Only the most intelligent and creative puzzle-solvers—say the top ten percent—will be capable of solving this puzzle and picking up the money dispensed by the button on the wall.

Now imagine that a pair of identical twins arrive, and one walks into each of the two rooms. The first twin has studied logic and done similar kinds of puzzles as a hobby for most of his life. As a result, he has become a highly capable puzzle-solver, and will be able to solve the puzzle in under ten minutes. The second twin, however, does not have the same skills. He may be attractive, fit, well-read, and talented in all variety of other ways, but he never took the time to learn puzzles the way that his brother did. As a result, he will not be able to push the button.

In terms of morality and justice, this situation seems rather unremarkable. The first twin "earned" his outcome through years of practice and effort, which the second twin did not. Because of this, the outcome seems fair. It feels just that the first twin gets all the money, while the second gets none.

But imagine we tweak the situation slightly. Suppose that instead of identical twins, the two individuals are unrelated to each other. Neither has chosen to spend any amount of time with puzzles, so all differences in puzzle-solving ability are inherited in some fashion, rather than earned by the individual through study. As in the first scenario, let us suppose that these two individuals achieve disparate outcomes: the occupant of room one is able to solve the puzzle relatively quickly, through some innate ability, while the occupant of room two simply cannot solve the puzzle. The occupant of room one walks away with his pockets overflowing with cash. The occupant of room two walks away empty-handed. The question is the following: is this outcome fair?

The situation appears to pose a moral conundrum. On the one hand, it might look as though the outcome is fair. After all, it is right for people to be rewarded for their virtues, and the relevant virtue in this scenario was puzzle-solving ability. The occupant of room one was rewarded for his competence, never mind its source, and the occupant of room two received the appropriate reward for lacking the relevant skill in this circumstance.

On the other hand, it can also be observed that neither of these individuals earned their skill. Neither individual studied puzzles, nor could they have known that they should have studied puzzles. Given these parameters, rewarding or punishing their skill (or lack thereof) seems arbitrary. Both individuals simply inherited their innate ability, so how can they be held responsible for their success or their failure? They could not choose how they were born, so it seems that the outcome is the result of genetic luck; an accident of birth. If this is the case, then the outcome is clearly unfair.

Which conclusion is correct? It is not yet clear. You probably have a feeling that it would be wrong not to reward the individual whose natural talents assisted him in completing the puzzle. After all, skill is skill, regardless of how it was acquired. But this feeling may be in competition with another intuition, that there is something unfair about the arbitrary nature of the outcome. This is because the source of the two individuals' abilities cannot be accounted for by looking at their own decisions. Neither the competence of the winning individual, nor the incompetence of the losing individual, was in any meaningful sense *earned*. This puzzle room shows how, from the individual perspective, our desire to create a society with fair and predictable outcomes for valued skills can be at odds with our desire to acknowledge responsibility.

The question becomes even more complicated when we look at the differing results of accepting the incentives-based perspective and the responsibility-based perspective. If we give precedence to social incentives, then we are rewarding skill and punishing incompetence. Overall, this is good for society, but it appears to be committing an injustice. If we give priority to responsibility, we avert the injustice of arbitrary punishment and reward, but we will fail to reward many virtues that are important, and we may even fail to punish vices that are harmful to others, and society may suffer tremendously. After all, if an individual was a pedophile or a violent psychopath by mere accident of birth, how could it be fair to punish them for what they did not choose? No matter how harmful their behavior may be, it would be an injustice to punish them for how they were born.

From the perspective of any given individual, it is hard to see a definitive answer as to whether incentives or responsibility is more important. I believe that this subject is actually at the heart of the modern political debate—although the sides are not clearly "left" versus "right," as we shall see. And far from being a matter of hypotheticals, the real-world stakes are quite high. To give you an idea of what I am talking about, consider a few modern examples of this kind of conflict.

The following essay was written for *Slate* in 2013, and given the straightforward title "If You Send Your Kid to Private School, You Are a Bad Person[13]":

---

[13] Benedikt, Allison. "If You Send Your Kid to Private School, You Are a Bad Person." *Slate.* 29 Aug, 2013. http://amp.slate.com/articles/double_x/doublex/2013/08/private_school_vs_public_school_only_bad_people_send_their_kids_to_private.html

...it seems to me that if every single parent sent every single child to public school, public schools would improve. This would not happen immediately. It could take generations. Your children and grandchildren might get mediocre educations in the meantime, but it will be worth it, for the eventual common good. [...]

Everyone needs to be invested in our public schools in order for them to get better. Not just lip-service investment, or property tax investment, but real flesh-and-blood offspring investment...

Benedikt argues that the present school system needs to be improved, but cannot be improved without flesh-and-blood investment. Her complaint is that rich families who can afford better schools are the source of political power in improving the schools, and by withdrawing their children from the broken system and putting them into private schools, they are also withdrawing all motivation to fix the public school system. She grants that a public education may not suit your child's needs completely, but if you are the sort of parent who can afford to send your child to private school, then your love and attention will make up for their bad education, and they'll be just fine. A poor public education for your child in the short run is worth it for the improvement for everyone later down the road.

Why would Benedikt care so much about the quality of public schools if being a good parent could more than make up for what was lost in a bad education? Because not everyone gets good parents. It was only by luck that you happened to have had good parents, while *everyone* gets access to public education. This is why she makes it a moral issue, rather than a mere calculation for maximizing the public good: if you act as if you deserve what you have inherited, you are not merely wrong—*you are a bad person.* By allowing for the unequal treatment of people based on their circumstances of birth, you are allowing for injustice.

Slate is a left-leaning publication, but identifying this conflict and criticizing personal loyalties is not just a left-wing issue. *Reason* published a short essay with a libertarian perspective called "The Hereditary Aristocracy of Citizenship[14]," in which Ilya Somin argued that, on principle, Americans strongly reject the legal privileges of aristocracy, but that we are not consistent in our principles. Citizenship, Somin argues, is a specially privileged legal class that is similar to the aristocracies of old:

> *Citizenship represents the most significant class lottery remaining in the modern world. The cover of your passport speaks volumes about your prospects for enjoying peace, prosperity, and happiness over the course of your life [...] Citizenship, in short, is massively consequential, and there's almost nothing meritorious about it. If you've spent your life as an American citizen, your* fortunes *have* depended *to a great extent upon inherited pedigree." [Quote from Rachel Lu] [...]*
>
> *Both old-style aristocracy and the modern aristocracy of citizenship forced many people into*

---

[14] Somin, Ilya. "The Hereditary Aristocracy of Citizenship." *Reason.* 7 July, 2018.
http://reason.com/volokh/2018/07/07/the-hereditary-aristocracy-of-citizenshi

poverty and oppression based largely on circumstances of birth. And, in their heyday, both systems commanded widespread support because they were seen as just a "natural" part of life that most people took for granted. But, in reality, both types of hereditary privilege were not naturally occurring facts of the world, but rather were (and are) enforced by large-scale government coercion. [...]

Today, we are repulsed by our ancestors who thought that it was perfectly normal – and unavoidable – that lords enjoyed an array of privileges denied to commoners and serfs. But few question our own hereditary privileges.

Aristocracy is a legal inequality between two people within the same nation. Citizenship, on the other hand, is a legal inequality between people of two different nations. In spite of this legal difference, Somin is saying that at a moral level, aristocracy and citizenship are really pretty similar, perhaps even identical. In his view, it isn't right to prefer one's own countrymen to foreigners, because it was only an accident of birth that you were born as a citizen of this country, rather than a citizen of somewhere else. In his view, we ought to "broaden access to citizenship, or reduce the extent of privileges associated with citizenship status." Or, he adds, some combination of the two.

As with Benedikt, Somin is making a moral argument, rather than appealing to our sense of rational self-interest or economic optimization. He is saying that citizenship, like aristocracy, is inherently unfair, and therefore unjust. You were only a citizen of a high-income, high-standard of living country by accident of birth. You did not earn it, and so you do not deserve the rewards of citizenship any more than anyone else.

Perhaps the most popular example of this kind of conflict, however, comes from an older essay. In 1989, Peggy McIntosh wrote "White Privilege: Unpacking the Invisible Knapsack[15]," in which she laid out the influential argument which would shape academic culture for decades to come:

> *Thinking through unacknowledged male privilege as a phenomenon, I realized that, since hierarchies in our society are interlocking, there was most likely a phenomenon of white privilege that was similarly denied and protected. As a white person, I realized I had been taught about racism as something that puts others at a disadvantage, but had been taught not to see one of its corollary aspects, white privilege, which puts me at an advantage. [...]*
>
> *We usually think of privilege as being a favored state, whether earned or conferred by birth or luck. Yet some of the conditions I have described here work systematically to overempower certain groups. Such privilege simply confers dominance because of one's race or sex.*
>
> *I want, then, to distinguish between earned strength and unearned power conferred systemically. Power from unearned privilege can*

---

[15] McIntosh, Peggy. "White Privilege: Unpacking the Invisible Knapsack." *Peace and Freedom Magazine.* Aug 1989. https://nationalseedproject.org/white-privilege-unpacking-the-invisible-knapsack

look like strength when it is in fact permission to escape or to dominate. [...]

Although systemic change takes many decades, there are pressing questions for me and I imagine for some others like me if we raise our daily consciousness on the perquisites of being light-skinned. What will we do with such knowledge? As we know from watching men, it is an open question whether we will choose to use unearned advantage to weaken hidden systems of advantage, and whether we will use any of our arbitrarily awarded power to try to reconstruct power systems on a broader base.

As in the previous two essays, McIntosh is saying that because your race is just a matter of luck, it is not right that people reap any rewards for being of a certain race. No harmful action needs to have been proven; the inequality *is* the injustice. If your own race has received benefits, for any reason, then she argues that you have a moral obligation to correct this difference. In this particular case, she is pointing the finger at whites, living as she does in a white society, but such a paper could just as plausibly be written in any other country that was built by, and for, a particular culture. If, for example, the paper had been written in Japan, then it may very well have been called "Japanese Privilege." The moral justification for such an argument would be identical, after all.

All three of these essays see the puzzle-room outcome as unfair. Because the source of inequality was not earned, many people (including Benedikt, Somin, and McIntosh) believe that equality should be the default. In the name of equality, they would have you put the well-being of other people's children over the well-being of your own children. They would have you abandon your nation and fellow citizens in favor of foreigners. They would even have you condemn your race as morally evil because the privileges and legacy that you would inherit from your race are not universal.

Having read about the Anwei, I hope you can see now that birth is no accident. It was not luck that brought your parents together: they each *chose* each other. Nor was it by luck that you happened to inherit the traits and culture of your parents. You could not have been anyone other than yourself, any more than you could now trade bodies with another person. Think of the puzzle-room: who these two individuals are is the result of the accumulated choices of their respective ancestors, who may have made tremendous sacrifices, or may have endured tremendous suffering and Darwinian selective pressures (i.e., painful deaths in the lineage, possibly on a large scale) to foster the skills and proclivities these two occupants now benefit from. Going back into the past, it is possible that the room-one individual's grandfather carefully selected his wife based upon her intelligence and creativity, and their resultant son chose his spouse based upon a similar basis for selection. Or perhaps the room-one individual's ancestors ten generations back were struck by some environmental calamity which killed all but the most resourceful and clever. It is hard to call such a scenario "good luck," but when such a tragedy results in a descendant being marginally better at puzzle-solving, and that descendant is able to win some money as a result, we consider it to be exactly that.

Put in even more basic terms, the condemnation of equality applies even in the case of the twins, where we intuitively believe the outcome was just because the one twin "earned" his skill through long periods of training. It is the action of sacrifice that makes us think that the achievement of the preferred outcome is fair. Therefore, it is not his present self who is being rewarded, but his *past* self who made the sacrifice of time and energy. Yet in the case of the unrelated puzzlers, sacrifices of time and energy *were still made*! Even if they were not made by the individual in room one himself, they were nevertheless made for him. Denying the justice of the puzzle-room outcome, therefore, is not so much an injustice to the individual as it is an injustice to his ancestors who made the sacrifices and choices that gave him his skill. It is an injustice, in other words, to the Anwei. The seemingly absent responsibility for the inequality in the puzzle-room *can* be located.

The idea that birth is somehow accidental, that it is fundamentally a matter of luck, simply does not hold up. It does not hold up even in the context of a thought experiment. The premise that we could have been born in a different body misunderstands the very nature of what a human being is. By contrast, recognizing the inseparability of "you" from the circumstances of your birth resolves the confusion of the puzzle room, as well as its real-world iterations. These arguments that say that you must treat your children like anyone else, and condemn your nation and race, are all based on a lie.

You ought to be kind to others, and respectful of other nations and cultures. But this respect and kindness are owed to your own identity first and foremost. Even the respect and kindness you show to others outside of your own identity are obligations to the Anwei, because it is honorable to be hospitable and respectable, and your actions will reflect on your family and your nation. You should be polite and decent to others so as to set a respectable and admirable example for your descendants and for others. No appeal to fictional hypotheticals is required to justify the importance of hospitality and common decency.

But let me return to the idea of equality and its advocates. Where did such an idea come from, and why has it become so prevalent? The fact that its adherents span the political divide should make it clear that the problem does not stem from ordinary right-versus-left politics. It comes from philosophy, and from one philosopher in particular.

Like people, ideas have lineages, and all of these positions are ideological descendants of John Rawls.

VI. The Failure of Ignorance

John Rawls was one of the most influential philosophers of the late 20th century, and it is his most famous book, *A Theory of Justice*, that matters to us here.

Rawls begins his argument with the observation that we think of "justice" as something absolute. We tend to dislike the idea of suspending the rules of justice for utilitarian ends ("the greater good"), and this observation is critical to understanding what, exactly, justice is. So where does this uncompromising notion of justice come from? Is it from an idea? Perhaps from a part of our neurological wiring?

For Rawls, the source of the absolute quality of justice is a belief that individuals are "inviolable," that all of us are, for all intents and purposes, sacred:

> ...*Each person possesses an inviolability founded on justice that even the welfare of society as a whole cannot override. For this reason, justice denies that the loss of freedom for some is made right by a greater good shared by others. It does not allow that the sacrifices imposed on a few are outweighed by the larger sum of advantages enjoyed by many. Therefore in a just society the liberties of equal citizenship are taken as settled; the rights secured by justice are not subject to political bargaining or to the calculus of social interests. The only thing that permits us to acquiesce in an erroneous theory is the lack of a better one; analogously, an injustice is tolerable only when it is necessary to avoid an even greater*

injustice. Being first virtues of human activities, truth and justice are uncompromising. [16]

In essence, Rawls says that the source of our sense of justice is the feeling that other individuals are special in some way. Because of this feeling, we should not harm people or deprive them of their freedom for simple utilitarian gains, even if many people would benefit. And because everyone possesses this "inviolability" in equal measure, we are all morally equal with each other. The absolute inviolability of an individual is the source of the intensity of our convictions about justice.

However, Rawls observed that most political systems designed to dispense justice just so happened to benefit those who advocated for them. The King would advocate for a political system with a single, all-powerful figurehead and ruler; the priest might prefer a political system in which religious piety was the predominant value, and political power was held by the teachers of religious doctrine; the laborer, for a political system that elevates the common man, where everything is decided by vote, and "experts" are regarded with suspicion. This tendency of personal bias makes it difficult to objectively judge whether a political system is fair or unfair, and a biased system of justice will not respect the inviolability of the individual. To get around this problem of motivated reasoning, Rawls introduced a thought experiment

[16] Rawls, John. *A Theory of Justice.* Cambridge, MA: Harvard University Press, 1971. 3. Web.
http://www.consiglio.regione.campania.it/cms/CM_POR
TALE_CRC/servlet/Docs?dir=docs_biblio&file=BiblioCont
enuto_3641.pdf

known as the *veil of ignorance,* also known as the "original position." This thought-experiment invites you to imagine that you are looking down on Earth, as though from the moon or from another dimension, through the eyes of a disembodied spirit. Looking down at the cities and towns of the planet, you have the power to choose which society you would like to live in, but without knowledge of which body within that society you will inhabit. Without knowledge of who you will become, you can decide if a society is fair objectively, free from the problem of motivated reasoning:

> *This original position is not, of course, thought of as an actual historical state of affairs, much less as a primitive condition of culture. It is understood as a purely hypothetical situation characterized so as to lead to a certain conception of justice. Among the essential features of this situation is that no one knows his place in society, his class position or social status, nor does any one know his fortune in the distribution of natural assets and abilities, his intelligence, strength, and the like. I shall even assume that the parties do not know their conceptions of the good or their special psychological propensities. The principles of justice are chosen behind a veil of ignorance.*
>
> *This ensures that no one is advantaged or disadvantaged in the choice of principles by the outcome of natural chance or the contingency of social circumstances. Since all are similarly situated and no one is able to design principles to favor his particular condition, the principles of justice are the result of a fair agreement or bargain.*

For given the circumstances of the original position, the symmetry of everyone's relations to each other, this initial situation is fair between individuals as moral persons, that is, as rational beings with their own ends and capable, I shall assume, of a sense of justice. The original position is, one might say, the appropriate initial status quo, and thus the fundamental agreements reached in it are fair.[17]

Rawls believed that two conclusions followed from this perspective. The first conclusion is that a just society will maximize liberty for all of its members. What does Rawls mean by "liberty?" The answer is not as obvious as it may sound, because "liberty" is as much a feeling as it is a legal concept. It can refer to either the ability of a group to act in its own interests, or it can mean the freedom of an individual from constraints, including constraints that may be imposed by the Anwei. I have included a relevant essay at the end of this letter specifically addressing the modern misuses of "liberty," which often mistakenly claim to speak on behalf of the American founding fathers by confusing these two meanings[18]. From the context in this instance, I believe Rawls is referring to the freedom of the individual, rather than the freedom of the group. Based on what I have described to you so far about the Anwei, this may be a little troubling. It is fairly common in academic circles to hear family and tradition described as "oppressive" to the individual because of the obligations they impose. We usually

---

[17] Ibid, 11.
[18] Appendix A

believe that justice includes paying what we owe, and if our very existence was the result of other people's choices and sacrifices, then freeing ourselves from any obligations we may have to those people is not particularly just. But this view is not uncommon among academics and intellectuals, and was not unique to Rawls.

The second conclusion is that the just society will only tolerate social and economic inequality to the degree that the worst off are made better off than they would have been under absolute equality. By this, Rawls means that sometimes, inequality drives advancement in progress and social welfare for all. If some degree of economic and social inequality coincides with improvements in the lives of the poorest and most socially isolated members of society, then in his view, this inequality—and *only* this inequality—is permissible. This idea that inequality should be rejected as unjust by default may sound familiar from the previous chapter. It is the primary contribution of Rawls to political philosophy, and the keystone of modern "social justice" movements that aim for equality.

As I have shown you, there are already good reasons to take issue with this conclusion. Neglecting the responsibility of others for the outcomes in our own lives is its own kind of injustice—namely, ungratefulness. To expect equality by default in our social, economic, and political strengths and weaknesses is to misunderstand what a human being is, and how we come to exist. But there are other consequences to this belief as well.

Think about a society that only tolerated inequality to the degree that it benefits the least well-off. Such a society has an established expectation of equality by default, rather than the more natural default of inequality. This is exactly the default you would expect if your starting point for seeking an objective theory of justice *presumes* equality, as the veil of ignorance does. But if his conclusion is accepted, it marks a change of legal importance. Up until the past few decades, those who demanded equality were required to prove some grievance or unlawful manipulation to justify a corrective redistribution. Under the moral and metaphysical presumption of equality, however, the burden of proof is lifted up from the resentful, and placed firmly on the shoulders of those who must now ask permission to be different. Beneath this standard, the alleged victim does not need to prove an *act of injustice* has been committed; he has only to assert that there is a difference, which implies—by default—a *state of injustice*. The beneficiaries of a unique legacy must prove a greater social good in order to justify their differentiation.

Under Rawls' veil of ignorance, a father's desire to leave an inheritance for his son is not admitted by default because inheritance often results in social and economic inequalities. This inheritance must be justified, and the justification *cannot be grounded in the father's love for his own son.* Love by itself is not a valid motivation under the veil of ignorance. Rather, it must be grounded in the benefit that his preferences for his own child might have for those who are the least well-off in society. In this way, "justice" as implemented through the veil of ignorance makes us impersonal and inhuman to those closest to us.

We can see this effect at work in the examples from the previous chapter. If your child could have been any other child, then it is unfair—and unjust—to put the wellbeing of your own child's education over the education system as a whole. As a platonic form of a person, you do not truly have any attachments to anyone else, so why should you care about your own child more than the child of a stranger? It is rational, even logical, to send your child to a public school, even at the risk of bullying and of hurting your child's social and educational development. Never mind what effect that may have on your child's thoughts about you as a parent, and their certainty about your love for them. They too— if they are being "fair"—will recognize that they could have been born into any family, and that there is no real reason to care more about you and your opinions than about any other adult. There is no reason to presume a commonality of likeness, interest, affection, inheritance, or destiny, because that has been defined off the table.

If it truly is an accident of birth that you happened to be an American citizen, rather than a citizen of Nicaragua, Algeria, or Japan, then it is morally indefensible to stand by the arbitrary privileges of citizenship, should citizens from those countries wish to come to the United States. The fact that the shared historical experiences, civic inheritances, languages, habits, traditions, infrastructural benefits, geographic interests, and genetics group certain populations together into natural nations is of no moral or legal significance if anyone could have been anyone else.

And if your race happens to have created an integrated system of law, culture, and language designed to make life better for you, then that system must be torn down, and your race condemned for the injustice inherent in such a project. Because it is only by arbitrary luck that you happened to be Anglo-American, and not some other race. As President Barack Obama once said, *you didn't build that*.

Under the veil of ignorance, the Anwei is inconceivable. Suicide can only be imagined as a byproduct of mental disorder and depression. Death is a horrible demon lurking on the margins, to be exorcised with transhumanism, distractions, and anti-aging products. Happiness is a product of socio-economic status, bought with stuff, and achieved on a grand scale with proper macro-economic policy. We are all valuable as individuals, *to* all individuals, despite there being more than seven billion of us.

This destruction of intimacy is bad enough, but I don't believe it is the only cost to accepting this dehumanizing perspective. People are willing to build legacies because they are personally motivated to do so. If the personal attachments which compel us to work for the future are categorized as morally invalid, then the engine of legacy itself is undermined. Pulling at the thread of equality unravels the long and beautiful tapestry that is civilization. In misunderstanding what a human being is, and designing a framework of objective justice for a sort of being that is not human, Rawls' veil of ignorance has sown the seeds of inhuman and unjust ideas which violently oppose our most basic moral instincts.

§

I hope I have been successful in showing you not only *that* Rawls was wrong in his conclusion, but also *why* Rawls was wrong. This is usually sufficient to reject an idea. However, if you are to go anywhere in your own intellectual journey, it will serve you best to seek out *how* a claim was wrong—how was the idea arrived at? What circumstances and other ideas led to its formation? Only by understanding the *how* can you fully comprehend anything. Where ideas are concerned, understanding its history and origins will help you discern whether it is partially wrong, or fundamentally wrong. No idea that becomes popular is ever entirely wrong, and it is important to give credit where credit is due, so as to avoid becoming an ideologue and missing out on something valuable.

So let me start with the argument itself. There are two places that an argument can go wrong: its premises, and its logic. We have seen that the two conclusions of Rawls' argument are actually unjust, especially his second conclusion in which he proposed that equality ought to be the social and economic default. Therefore, either his premises must be wrong, or somewhere on the line between his premises and his conclusion, there was a confusion or a mistake.

Rawls begins with the premise that justice and fairness are synonymous. I believe this seemingly obvious observation is actually a rather brilliant and accurate starting point, because we often think of justice as something lofty and abstract. Fairness, however, is no abstract philosophical construct. I have learned this in part from watching toddlers; one of their first and favorite phrases is "that's not fair!" Even monkeys possess a sense of fairness, and will reject food if another monkey receives a better food reward for performing the same task[19]. What is fair in a certain context may be learned, but we seem to come with the concept of "fairness" built into us. If it were otherwise, monkeys would not be able to demonstrate the intuitive sense of fairness which they possess, since they lack abstract theories on the nature of justice.

Entire books have been written on the origins, nature, and essence of justice. They discuss natural law, social contracts, utilitarianism, categorical imperatives, and other abstract theories, but ultimately, these are all just expansions upon what people like you and me *intuitively feel* is just. To understand the basics of justice, all of these theories are unnecessary. Most people have a good understanding of what justice is intuitively, and do not need complicated moral and ethical philosophies to know that it is wrong to lie, cheat, steal, rape, or murder, that we ought to give people the benefit of the doubt, to reciprocate the behaviors of others, and to reject unwarranted double-standards. These core principles make up the foundation of "justice." Most of the disagreements beyond that are about applications. This is not to say that these theories are worthless. They are established so that when dealing with problems where our intuitions give us no clear answers, the theory may show us a fair solution. In

---

[19] Brosnan, Sarah and de Waal, Frans. "Monkeys reject unequal pay." *Nature*, 18 Sept, 2003. https://www.nature.com/articles/nature01963.

new or complicated situations, these theories can be quite useful. In most cases, however, the complicated theories are unnecessary to determine what is or is not just in a particular situation. Rawls' starting premise is correct: justice is fairness. The error must be somewhere else.

After defining justice as fairness, Rawls observed that our sense of fairness has an absolute quality that does not allow for bartering or compromise. For instance, we tend to grimace at the idea of sacrificing someone's life for a "general good," or at sacrificing a little bit of justice in order to gain a lot of wealth. Rawls infers that this sense of absoluteness comes from a natural belief that individuals are special, or "inviolable." If personal inviolability is the source of the absoluteness of our sense of justice, he argues that the best way to respect individual inviolability is to act as if we could have been anyone else—the veil of ignorance. And from the veil of ignorance, he believes that his two conclusions about liberty and equality are what everyone would choose.

We could summarize his argument in the following manner:

1. Justice is fairness
2. Justice is a universal, intuitive emotion
3. Intuitive emotion says that justice is absolute
4. The absolute quality of justice comes from individual inviolability
5. Individual inviolability is maximized through *veil of ignorance*
6. The just society is a society that people would choose to live in from the *veil of ignorance*

7. The just society maximizes individual liberty and permits no inequality which does not benefit the least well off

If point (1) is correct, and point (7) is wrong, then the error must be somewhere in between. Point (2) is correct if point (1) is accepted, because fairness is a universal, intuitive emotion. Point (3) is slightly more contentious, but I believe to be correct.

Point (4) is where I believe the error rests—the idea that we believe individuals to be in some sense sacred or "inviolable." Remember:

...Each person possesses an inviolability founded on justice that even the welfare of society as a whole cannot override.

This description does capture the absolute quality that most people have of the concept of justice. But the explanation Rawls posits—a sense of individual "inviolability"—does not hold up. If justice was derived from respect for the inviolability of the individual, then societies which did not respect individual rights would not be able to produce just societies, but this is not the case.

Most all of human history was dominated by "honor cultures." In an honor-culture, individuals are not thought of as having intrinsic worth. They are seen as members of a group, and of having value based upon the value which they provide to the group. The modern Western world is a "dignity culture," where individuals are assumed to have intrinsic worth, and it is easy to believe that this dignity culture is the basis of justice because it has become the popularly held foundation for justice, but honor can also serve as a foundation. The individualism beneath our dignity culture is the product of the Enlightenment, only a few centuries ago. Justice has been discussed by philosophers, poets, and statesmen since the days of Ancient Greece. In fact, one of the earliest allusions to a higher concept of justice was in Sophocles' play *Antigone*, in which the female protagonist chooses to bury her dead brother, even though she knew that doing so was a crime punishable by death. When asked why she defied the king's orders, she said that there was a higher law than that of the king, a natural order which obliged her to properly bury the dead. This assertion of a higher law, which forms part of the basis of the Western common law tradition, does not require any particular respect for individuality. The concept is never mentioned, and simply is not needed.

Philosopher Tamler Sommers even argues that honor cultures can be *more* just than dignity cultures because they respect the care we have for our own sense of honor, a value which is grounded in the same intuitions as justice itself. Honor cultures can also allow conflicts to be resolved in a more personal and satisfying fashion, whereas dignity cultures will ultimately require a "Leviathan"—a powerful and impartial state—to intervene and resolve our conflicts on our behalf[20]. This intervention is not only less satisfying than a more personal resolution, but can even deprive us of the chance to make amends with those who have wronged us. I have included an

---

[20] Sommers, Tamler. *Why Honor Matters*. New York, NY: Basic Books, May 2018. Print.

elaborative essay I have written on the subject of conflict, resolution, and relationships at the end of this letter, which explains in more detail why third-party intervention can actually rob us of deeper relationships[21]. Suffice to say, the fact that just societies can exist which do not respect the concept of "individual inviolability" proves that Rawls' foundation for justice is wrong.

I will go even further than this: it is strange to presume that our intuitions about justice come from a sense of individual inviolability when one of the oldest crimes against justice was that of *hubris*. Hubris is an old Greek word for the supreme kind of arrogance: pride in the face of the Gods. The arrogant, hubristic person does not believe he needs anyone else. He believes that he is better than everyone else. He believes that he is "inviolable." He may even believe that he is God. He is, in a sense, the logical end point of individualistic idealism; a sort of mocking caricature of what one of the most famous and well-known intellectuals of my time, Dr. Jordan Peterson, has referred to as the "divine individual[22]." "Individual inviolability" is, in and of itself, an inherently arrogant presumption. It is entitled and ungrateful, and will inevitably bring about what always follows hubris: *nemesis*—divine retribution.

So let me return to the source of the absolute feeling of justice that Rawls described. The fact that most justice cultures were honor-based, rather than

[21] Appendix B.
[22] Peterson, Jordan. "My New Year's Letter to the World." Jordan B. Peterson, 31 Dec, 2016. Web. https://jordanbpeterson.com/philosophy/new-years-letter/

dignity-based, proves that this intuition of inviolability has its origins in ideology, not in primordial human nature itself. The fact that this sense of individual inviolability can cause problems, undermining our expectations of honor and humility, shows that the divine individual is not a particularly just idea in its own right. But most importantly, you can simply observe that individuals aren't "divine" or "inviolable" in an objective fashion. Some of them will be intensely special to you, but most people simply don't matter. Some people, by their nature, or because of something they've done, seem to *deserve* destruction and erasure—traitors and those who sexually abuse children, for instance. If this sense of inviolability can be lost, then in what sense was it there to begin with?

§

I believe that the feeling of primacy captured in Rawls' description of justice is entirely explainable without appealing to individual inviolability. Our sense of justice comes from the human yearning for *stability*.

I am not saying that justice and stability are the same, but that stability is the experiential goal and measure of justice. I'm sure that you have experienced the suffering of disappointed expectations by now, or of feeling as though the world is outside of your control. Often times, this feeling of powerlessness is not caused by a deficiency of power *per se*, but by an inability to see what is going to happen. We need some semblance of stability in order to build anything complex, and to plan for the future. If the objects around us have no solidity to them, then nothing will stay the same as we attempt to adjust and adapt ourselves to improve our lives. Without the ability to plan for the future, we become anxious and uncertain. Our autonomic nervous system will dominate our prefrontal cortex, and we will become the slaves of adrenaline and cortisol, rather than agents of consciousness, problem-solving, and creation.

The elaborate edifice of civilization cannot stand without *something* stable to rest on, be it a myth, a nation, a religion, an idea, or merely a king. Life itself cannot last without its constituent parts remaining generally the same across time: if our bones, cells, and organs were constantly changing into something else entirely, or dissolving, then we could not be. Our body parts *are* constantly changing, as I described before, but their identity remains unchanged, in spite of their constant evolution. Like a river, they are stable, even in motion.

Human beings, however, are complicated and shifty creatures, the most versatile of all animals. Being around other people is an inherently unstable situation. How can we live when our surrounding family and friends, when our very *self*, may very well be members of the most chaotic and unpredictable entities in the universe?

"Justice" was the human solution to the problem of human chaos. Justice imposes predictability on others by establishing boundaries around what people are allowed to do, and punishing, expelling, or killing those who transgress those boundaries. It is good to be able to do what you want, but it more important to prevent other people from doing bad things to you, or things which you otherwise couldn't predict that could harm you. After all, there are more of "them" than there are of you, and at least one of them is bound to be stronger, smarter, or more brutal than you are. So we came up with rules, enforced by the majority, which prohibited murder, theft, rape, and forms of harmful deception. By assenting to these rules, we gave up some of our freedom in exchange for some stability in the behavior of others. It was this exchange, and the effectiveness of its implementation, that made cities, civilization—perhaps all forms of socialization—possible.

Usually, justice is discussed in terms of distributing welfare, protecting freedom, and cultivating virtue. Still, in all three of these goals is the ideal of stability and predictability. We don't just want a system that distributes welfare fairly; we want a system in which we know what we can expect, based upon what we do. We don't just want freedom; we want to know which freedoms we possess and which we don't. We don't just want to be virtuous; we want to know which traits are held to be virtuous. If these things are unknown to us or are changing too quickly, then we will not feel like we are living in a fair society.

This understanding of justice—not only as fairness, but also as a yearning for stability—explains the sense of primacy which Rawls alludes to. Any exception made in a system of justice for a short-term gain will introduce by precedent the possibility of future exceptions. What might change tomorrow? How can we know that people will behave in a fashion that won't destroy the plans laid out yesterday? Society cannot work without some constraint around the chaos of humanity. This is why justice—not based around a sense of "individual inviolability," but coming from a desire for stability—holds it impermissible to hurt the few for the benefit of the many. If such an action undermined the law itself, then the benefit to the many would quickly disappear anyway. There is no mechanism available to maintain the fruits of injustice.

§

I have been belaboring the error of Rawls to you at some length now, which may seem particular, perhaps even personal. In truth, Rawls is not the source of this problem. He is really just the latest iteration of an older idea. I told you that ideas have lineages, and that Rawls was in many ways the father of the arguments offered by Benedikt, Somin, and McIntosh in the previous chapter. In the same manner, Rawls' thoughts on justice can trace his lineage back to older ideas.

In *A Theory of Justice*, Rawls cites Immanel Kant as one of his primary moral influences. In the philosophical world, it's a respectable place to start: Kant was probably one of the most brilliant thinkers ever to live. A moral philosopher from Germany, Kant set about attempting to save free will from the mechanistic causality of David Hume[23]. In *Grounding for the Metaphysics of Morals*, Kant defined the will outside of the body and separate from the material

---

[23] Hume believed that a proper understanding of the laws of cause and effect logically precluded any belief in "free will." Because people believed that moral responsibility was grounded in choice, Hume's argument appeared to threaten morality itself.

world itself, thereby freeing it from the reach of mechanistic causality. But this divorce from reality did not make us more free. American philosopher Matthew Crawford argues that Kant's metaphysics of will resulted in a moral ethos which required people to take absolute responsibility for their behavior *regardless of circumstances and environment*[24]. Because who we are is largely determined by where we are, Kant's separation of the will from the body morally permitted the commodification of our attention. If the will has no relation to the real world, then we have no moral claim over our environment—the "attentional commons" as Crawford calls it—which molds us and guides us into becoming who we would *will* ourselves to be. Advertisers, casinos, social media companies, and other distractions and diversions have other plans for how we should spend our time. If we complain about it, then we are simply not taking responsibility for ourselves as we ought to.

The characteristic separation of mind and matter in the philosophies of both Kant and Rawls can be taken back even further, through Christian theology and all the way to Plato. I believe that the concept of "individual inviolability," for example, is actually Christian in origin. Christianity holds that all people are "image-bearers" of God, and, because God is sacred, all humans are sacred as well. Because we are all equal as image-bearers of God, and because God is the source and measure of all goodness, Christian theology holds that we are all equal to each other in Christ. Christianity holds that our bodies are not the

---

[24] Crawford, Matthew. *The World Beyond Your Head: on Becoming an Individual in an Age of Distraction.* New York, NY. Farrar, Straus & Giroux, 2016. Print.

same as our spirit, and while we can perfect our spirit and bring it closer to God through the use of the body, the body, in and of itself, is of little use or concern. The body and spirit are separate.

These ideas are very old and powerful, and cannot be dismissed quite as easily as Rawls and his veil of ignorance. There is much more to say about Christianity and Platonism—the ideological progenitor of Christianity—then I have described here, although I have included an essay on the subject of Christianity and identity at the end of this letter[25], should the subject interest you. Nevertheless, as a general rule, I would urge you to be wary and skeptical of those who claim that other worlds and dimensions supersede our own in importance, especially if they are absolutely certain in their own conviction. The subjects of "forms" and of heaven and hell are complicated and conceptually difficult, and those most adamantly assured of their truth are usually the least knowledgeable about the underlying reasons behind their own deeply held beliefs.

To bring this matter to a close, the ends of justice, good governance, and social harmony are not served by cutting human nature apart for the sake of simplicity. The body and soul are not separate, antagonistic entities, but components of a unified whole, just as human individuals can be component elements of a single lineage, or Anwei. There is certainly tension between the will and the world (including the body), just as there is often tension between individuals that are parts of the same family or tribe, or between the individuality of our

---

[25] Appendix C.

71

experience with the individuality of our *being*—how we feel versus what we are. But observing these occasional tensions is not proof of their essential disunity. It only shows that we live in a complicated and changing world, and in this complicated world, we see different and sometimes competing strategies for navigating the challenges it imposes upon us. How can we find moral responsibility without free will? How can we create a stable society if our fellow citizens are susceptible to motivated reasoning? These are challenges that philosophers, statesmen, judges, and ordinary people have struggled with for thousands of years, and there are no easy answers. But we do ourselves no favors by simplifying the human animal into something it is not, and then acting as if our model was reality.

In the end, reality is its own best model.

As with life and with our experience of life, we can make the most sense of justice and quandaries like the puzzle-room by remembering and aligning ourselves with the Anwei. The Anwei is not an all-encompassing solution to the challenge of creating a just society, but it is a solid foundation to build from. It prioritizes our loyalties in a manner that aligns with our natural intuitions about justice, and which builds up legacies, rather than destroying them. The Anwei is stable even when individual people are not, and so justice imagined through the lens of the Anwei is stable when justice for the individual is not. Because individuals receive gifts—and sometimes curses—from the past that they did not earn, it would seem that all of social life is in some sense unfair. From the perspective of the Anwei, however, this accumulation of benefits can be accounted for, and can therefore be fair.

Because of its stability and fairness, the Anwei is not just the path of life and purpose: it is also the path of justice.

VI. Becoming the Anwei

Dear grandchild, I hope it is clear to you through all of this how important it is that you know who and what you are, what benefits to yourself and to your family and society come from truly living as an integrated part of the Anwei, rather than trying to live for yourself as an isolated individual. But I expect you may be wondering how this can be done, perhaps even *if* it can be done. I hope I have shown through earlier examples that even if perfect unification with the Anwei is impossible, people can move closer and further away from its influence, as shown by the inhabitants of Loma Linda, of Okinawa, and of Sardinia, as well as by the relative spread found in the Harvard Study of Adult Development and the distance between the lives of musicians like Chester Bennington and Maynard James Keenan.

But it is still a challenge to figure out how we might improve the quality of connection with our ancestors, our unborn descendants, our family, and our greater societal circle which form the collective inheritance we are each a part of. In the world I grew up in, for example, most of society seemed purpose-built to break these ties, and draw me in to other attachments, either religious, political, geographical, or sub-cultural in nature.

The appeal was always to take up a cause, to lose oneself in an obscure genre of music, or to find "God" in an immaterial plane elsewhere. I don't list off these items to disparage them; all of these are in fact powerful tools of connection to the Anwei. But most of the young people I knew sought these out as replacements for connection to identity, and as escapes from their own family, culture, and faith. I suspect things are likely to be quite similar for you. Pushing back and living your own life in opposition to the inertia of the world can be like swimming upstream against a slow but steady current of a powerful river.

Nevertheless, I think you can learn to swim. It is a matter of technique, practice, and motivation. I have done all I can in previous chapters where motivation is concerned, and I cannot help you with practice, but I have cobbled together some lose ideas about the techniques of living in closer proximity with the Anwei. They are, unfortunately, incomplete, but they may move you in what I believe is the right direction, or inspire you to more precise and effective tools and strategies of your own devising.

Land

Historically, families and clans were tied to particular places. Rights to land[26] were traditionally claimed by virtue of having lived there a long time, which could be demonstrated by a clear history of use—"mixing one's labor with the land"—or by having ancestors buried there. Both reasons convey a kind of value in the form of connection with the Anwei: the latter allows us to commune with our

---

[26] It may be claimed that rights to land are determined by force, rather than moral justifications. But force is traditionally a tool of enforcing existing norms, not the mechanism for creating them. An equal or inferior power will often instigate violence with a superior one if a moral norm has been violated, which speaks to the primacy of the norm, rather than the primacy of force alone.

ancestors and to regularly remember them when we see their burial plots. It keeps them in our minds. The fact that they were often buried far away from the living areas (for hygiene and safety reasons) meant their graves sometimes doubled as boundary-markers, making them guardians of the land itself, even in death.

The value invested in the land also facilitated connection with ancestors and descendants, as the nature of your grandfathers could be felt in their creations. If a particular ancestor of yours had built a house or a water-mill, then you might be able to get a feeling of who those ancestors were through the quality of their construction. While repairing a stone wall once used to keep sheep inside, the thought might cross your mind: "my great-great-grandfather built this wall." As you become more proficient in masonry yourself, the peculiarities of the workmanship will become more apparent to you, and you will know your ancestors better as a result of taking on the same skills as they did, through the artifacts on the land they left behind.

Of course, this is not necessarily limited to land. Humans have always created artifacts that can be taken with them, and a knife, a piece of jewelry, a well-made coat, or an ornate quilt can all convey the same connective feeling as something more geographically fixed like a cottage or a dock.

But there is also a feeling from the environment itself; nature in one place, untamed by human hands. The Anwei is the product of interaction between humans and their environment, and when we leave the environment that shaped our ancestors, or change it sufficiently that it is no longer the same place that they lived, we also leave a part of them behind. This is not to say that you should live as a luddite, or move back to the steppe of Ukraine, where your Indo-European ancestors came from[27]. But you should not move away from the home of your parents and grand-parents lightly. They are your most direct connection to the Anwei, and you are unlikely to "find yourself" elsewhere in the world, among foreign cultures and peoples. The economic opportunities and excitement of travel are rarely worth the damage done to the continuity of the Anwei.

In short, living in the land of your ancestors and truly coming to understand it and be at home with it is one important and powerful way of bringing yourself closer to the Anwei, and reaping the rewards of its connection.

Myth and Family History

The genealogical sections of the great stories, like the Bible and the Iliad, are often thought of as boring for modern people, especially to modern young people like yourself. But there is still often times a genealogical section in the great epics, which survived in great part because they were exciting and enjoyable to their audience. Why would these "boring" sections be included? As these epics also contain magic and the miraculous, the mere documentation of history is not a likely explanation.

---

[27] Anthony, David. *The Horse, The Wheel, and Language: How Bronze-Age Riders from the Eurasian Steppes Shaped the Modern World.* Princeton, NJ. Princeton University Press, 2007. Print.

In generations past, stories were more geographically local, in their creation and in their retelling. They spoke of particular families in particular places that the audience was likely to be intimately familiar with. There was a very high chance that, if someone were to tell the story of the Iliad, your great-great grandfather's name might be listed among the ship captains of the second scroll, or among the Trojan allies fighting with Hector. At the very least, you would hear the name of the King under which your ancestor served. Your family, your genes, your Anwei were in the story, and so the story belonged to you, as well as to the other people whose ancestors participated in that war, Trojan or Achaean.

It is very plausible that genealogies may have been the *most* compelling and important parts of these epics, for the purpose of persuading the audience of the story's relevance. In establishing personal relevance, these stories helped establish the cultural wisdom, norms, shared myths, and eventually, the civilization that can follow from collective investment in these things. If you have a place in the myth, then you have a place in the society of the myth.

Today, I see many more myths, but fewer that give meaning and place to their audience. Fantasy, science-fiction, and "high literature" all establish culture, but they do so without attachment. They are impersonal and rootless.

One of the best modern exceptions to this trend is Harold Courlander's book *The African*, a story which is more popularly known in its plagiarized form: *Roots*, by Alex Haley[28].

Israeli historian Yuvan Noah Harari argues in his book *Sapiens*[29] that the creation of myths is one of our defining traits and most powerful abilities. It allowed us to organize into groups through the creation of trust, which Neanderthals and Cro-Magnons could not emulate. If Harari is correct on this point (as I believe he is), then the much-maligned political polarization of America reflects a breakdown of the myths that previously held us together.

Perhaps this is why the ancients hated blasphemy with such seriousness.

Children

It should be obvious to you—I hope—that for the sake of the Anwei, it is imperative that you have children if it is possible. Ideally, three or more, since populations begin to wane beneath a 2.1 children-per-family reproduction rate (two to replace the parents, and a bit extra to account for those who fail to reproduce).

But there are a number of people—among them celibates, homosexuals, and the infertile—who are highly unlikely to have children. These people, contrary to what you may initially assume, are not

---

[28] Lubasch, Arnold. "Roots Plagiarism Suit Is Settled." *New York Times*. 15 Dec, 1978. Web.
https://www.nytimes.com/1978/12/15/archives/roots-plagiarism-suit-is-settled-roots-plagiarism-suit-is-settled.html.
[29] Harari, Yuval Noah. *Sapiens*. New York, NY. Harper, 2011. Print.

genetic dead-ends and dead-weight. Often times, they are even the greatest contributors to the Anwei, in their accomplishments, artwork, thought, writing, music, and exploration.

The Anwei survives in a primarily linear fashion, but is not exclusively linear. If an individual member creates something of value which the others can benefit from, then they may in fact be strengthening the legacy and identity overall, despite not reproducing themselves. The evolutionary biologist J.B.S. Haldane more or less summarized the idea when he wrote that he would "gladly give up his life for two brothers or eight cousins[30]." One person who sacrifices their own procreative rights to work for the moderate benefit of their entire tribe can—in certain circumstances—actually provide more genetic advantage than if they were to have simply had children.

Of course, the mathematics of this are highly contextual and subject to diminishing returns. If everyone in a tribe devoted all of their energy into expanding their culture and power rather than having children, then there would be no tribe after a single generation. A future recipient generation is necessary for all that work to be meaningful.

It is also very easy for the childless to lose sight of this necessity, and to get so caught up in their own individualistic endeavors that they forget their place in the Anwei, and even become antagonistic towards it. This problem is not unique to the childless: even parents can live selfish lives which alienate their own children. But the allure is certainly greater for those

---

[30] This concept is known as the theory of "kin-selection" in evolutionary biology circles.

whose living legacy does not say "good morning" to them daily.

These unique challenges notwithstanding, there has always been a place for the childless within the Anwei. They have held roles as priests and shamans, laborers and soldiers, artists and scientists, as slaves and even as kings, and have been able to dedicate intense time and attention to tasks and problems which parents simply cannot. So long as parents are producing at least 2-3 children per couple, the childless members of the Anwei can be powerful and important aids in its survival and success.

If you are in any doubt whatsoever about which side of this divide you are to fall on, err on the side of children. Do not be deterred by talk of how expensive or time-consuming children can be, though they certainly can be both. My paternal grandparents had six children, and my maternal grandparents had eight. Though I'm sure this may have caused short-term challenges in time and money, both families reaped long-term rewards in companionship, satisfaction, purpose, and legacy that no amount of time or money could ever replace.

A final word on this subject: children are the products of their parents, yet many Americans have taken to intermarrying with unlike groups for no reason other than convenience and loneliness— loneliness which could have been avoided by maintaining connection with their own families and tribes. I think this has to do with moving around so much; a result of our disconnection with the land. Unfortunately, the children of these marriages look, think, and speak in a manner completely alien to any of their biological ancestors, with no realistic possibility of connection or of achieving that sense of belonging attained through aligning yourself with the Anwei. This is not an absolute argument against intergroup relationships, but an admonition not to do so lightly and thoughtlessly, without consideration of the cost such a dramatic merging can impose upon your children.

Ritual

We are all aware of the Western classics— Homer, Sophocles, Plutarch, Plato, Aristotle, the Bible, the Nordic sagas, the Arthurian Legends, Shakespeare, and many more. We are almost completely unaware, however, of the epics of China. The Book of Darkness, (黑暗傳 "Hēi Àn Zhuàn") for example, is roughly comparable to the biblical book of Genesis as a creation myth, and similar to the works of Homer in that it was likely preceded by some kind of oral tradition prior to being recorded sometime between the 7th and 10th century AD. The Records of the Grand Historian (太史公書 "Tàishǐgōng shū" or "Shiji"), the Book of Documents (書 "Shū"), and the Bamboo Annals (竹書紀年 "Zhúshū Jìnián") document the history of the Xia dynasty, circa 2070 – 1600 BC. Like Arthurian and Homeric legend, the Xia dynasty was a mysterious, quasi-mythological period that archeology is slowly beginning to uncover as more than mere story. These, and other myths, legends, histories, poetry, and court documents, comprise a written tradition comparable to any Western narrative collection in its stylistic sophistication, and perhaps even more comprehensive in scope.

What truly differentiates China from the West, however, is the universality of ritual. Ritual, in the broad sense, is merely a formalized habit. In the West ritual has a distinctly supernatural connotation, but this is not a necessary association for the term, as the dominant Chinese social philosophy since around 500 BC demonstrates.

Confucianism is an essentially humanistic doctrine, although some sociologists and anthropologists talk about it as a religion (and with good reason). Confucianism emphasizes social harmony, and accomplishes this through the encouragement of a kind of virtue ethics. One of these virtues was 禮/礼 "li," ritual propriety[31]. In one demonstrative instance, Confucius and his followers were preparing a sheep for sacrifice, but one of his disciples—Tsze-kung—thought that the sacrifice was unnecessary, and proposed keeping the sheep, rather than killing it. Confucious replied: "Tsze, you love the sheep; I love the ceremony."

Rituals are a form of habit, and habits are the most powerful agent in shaping who—and what—we are. Respect for one's family and elders (孝 "Xiao") being another virtue, the interweaving of "li" and "xiao" created a culture of ritualized social life that has lasted for thousands of years, and which even Communism—which destroyed or hid the ancient stories and family narratives during the horrific "Cultural Revolution"—was unable to completely

---

[31] The others include 仁 "Ren" (benevolence), 義/义 "Yi" (justice), 智 "Zhi" (knowledge), 信 "Xin" (integrity), 忠 "Zhong" (loyalty), 孝 "Xiao" (filial piety), and 節/节 "Jie" (contingency).

eradicate from the underlying national consciousness. Even without explicit knowledge of history, the Chinese even think differently than Westerners, looking to the context of an object rather than to the thing itself[32].

The implications of this are profound. For the Chinese people, the internalization of ritual has resulted in an *experience* of connection with the Anwei.

The importance of ritual is not a completely alien concept in the West. Aristotle said that "...these virtues are formed in man by his doing the action," which historian and writer William Durant summarized in the much-misattributed phrase: "We are what we repeatedly do. Excellence, then, is not an act, but a habit." But the religious application of ritual in our social life to be accepted and respected is not as strong as it once was. Since the rationalism of the Enlightenment, ritual has been derided as superstitious, inauthentic, or at best, superfluous. It has taken some time to gain traction, but today, most Westerners choose not to follow ritual propriety, nor do they respect their elders, and as a result, they are not connected to their Anwei.

What does all of this talk of ritual mean? It means—to start with—that you should take the time to remember birthdays and special holidays. Make these things priorities in your life, and organize your calendar around them. Take Thanksgiving and Christmas off, the way that the ancient Christians and Jews took the Sabbath off, and observe this family

---

[32] Nisbett, Richard E. *The Geography of Thought: How Asians and Westerners Think Differently ... and Why*. Free Press, 2004.

time *religiously*. Remember your anniversary (when you are married), and father's and mother's days, and plan for all of these in advance. If you can, take some time every day to meditate on the lives of your parents and siblings. If you become skillful in this, you may even learn to meditate on the lives of the dead and the unborn.

It has become nearly cliché to tell young people to "respect their elders," and the admonition is especially suspicious when it comes from the elderly in a self-serving context. Nevertheless, it is imperative that you respect your elders, and develop a meaningful relationship with them. This does not mean that you deferentially agree with and accept everything that they say, however, because that is not how you respect someone, nor is it how you foster a deep relationship. Respecting your elders means taking them seriously, and taking them seriously may mean disagreeing with them, even disagreeing in a heated manner.

Respecting the importance of ritual also means practicing the greater rituals of your culture. It is better, for example to get married in an official religious ceremony than it is to run off to the courthouse together. Grand ceremonies like marriage may seem esoteric and largely unnecessary, but they have developed over a long period of time, and it is not always easy to understand why certain aspects of a ritual are important or beneficial. But your own youthful incomprehension does not mean that there are no benefits. A writer I admire once made the analogy to electricity: very few people really understand how to wire a house, let alone how electricity works at a more fundamental level. But that doesn't mean that they cannot enjoy the benefits of turning on a light by flicking the switch. My wife and I were married in a Christian wedding, before an altar, with vows, after exchanging rings, and a concluding hand-fastening ceremony. Neither of us invented any of these rituals, although they were somewhat personalized in our case. More importantly, neither my wife nor I would be able to give a complete account of how or why such rituals are materially beneficial to ourselves or our marriage. But they are important. For example, consider just one aspect of the ceremony: family attendance. Dr. Randy Olson, the Lead Data Scientist at Life Epigenetics, takes a data-approach to marriage longevity, and had this to say:

> ...your wedding ceremony has a huge impact on the long-term stability of your marriage. Perhaps the biggest factor is how many people attend your wedding: Couples who elope are 12.5x more likely to end up divorced than couples who get married at a wedding with 200+ people. Clearly, this shows us that having a large group of family and friends who support the marriage is critically important to long-term marital stability.[33]

Religiosity (measured by frequency of church attendance) and motivation (caring about traditional characteristics in a spouse, rather than looks or wealth) were also high indicators of a successful

---

[33] Olson, Randal. ""What makes for a stable marriage?" *Randal S.* Olson. 10 Oct, 2014. Web. www.randalolson.com/2014/10/10/what-makes-for-a-stable-marriage/

wedding. Curiously, spending a lot of money on the wedding is associated with short-lived marriages, even though earning lots of money is associated with longer-lasting ones. And contrary to what unmarried skeptics like to believe, long-lasting marriages are, as a general rule, happy ones.

What ties all of these things together is that they are aligned with how traditional wedding ceremonies were conducted. You may not understand the reasons behind the rituals at first (which is not to say you should not try to understand them), but respect for tradition and ritual is one of the best ways to align yourself with the Anwei, and in doing so, to receive the benefits that it has accumulated for you personally.

Marriage

I would be remiss to write about weddings but neglect their object: marriage. Honesty compels me to be humble on this subject. As I write this, I myself have only been married for twenty-three months. However, both my parents and your grandmother's parents have each remained married for about thirty years—all still married to this day as I write to you. The following points, therefore, come not from experience, but from observation.

Marriage is the distilled essence of what living with the Anwei is about. It is the surrender of your own ego and desires, not to your spouse, but to the marriage itself. Marriage requires you to become someone other than who you might have wanted—or expected—to be when you were your own master. So far as I have observed, your marriage will succeed or fail depending on your willingness to become what it requires you to be.

This sounds like a serious loss of freedom because it is. Yet in spite of this sacrifice, millions of people voluntarily forgo the freedoms of individuality and enter the bonds of marriage every year. They do this because marriage is how they become who they were meant to be. It is the best way to live long, to remain healthy, to succeed generally, and to be happy.

Marriage is challenging, make no mistake. No matter who you think you are marrying at the altar, you will find that you are married to someone very different later on. Perhaps you will discover something about them that you did not know. Perhaps they undergo a dramatic change, or a series of minor changes that transform them into someone new. A new child, a new job, a new friend, or a new home can all have a transformative effect like this. Yet through this change, their identity to you and to the marriage remains the same. Hopefully, you too will be changing and growing as you become older, but your identity to your marriage will also remain.

If you believe that the marriage is about what is convenient for you, then this change may appear threatening or discomforting. Change has certainly led to many divorces over the past decade. But if you remember that it is you who is convenient for the marriage, then the change becomes not only tolerable, but exciting. For example, you may one day see your wife transformed before your eyes into a mother, or your husband transformed into a father. If your attention is on yourself, this change may be displeasing. But if your focus is on the marriage, then almost nothing is more beautiful.

A husband is, in a sense, not a person. Neither is a wife, a mother, or a father. They are roles, which individual people must take on, just as they once were children, and one day may become grandparents. William Wordsworth once said that "the child is the father of the man," meaning that who someone is in their youth will determine how they are in their older years. But is the child the same person as the man? As I discussed earlier, the answer is clearly "yes," though it may feel to you as though he has changed so much that he is no longer the same person. So too may a spouse appear to change as they adopt new roles, because the world still turns, even after your wedding day.

Neither you nor your spouse are stable—it is your marriage that gives you form and a meaningful identity to each other. Remember this, and succeed in marriage, and you will understand the Anwei.

§

These elementary tools—land, myth, children, ritual, and marriage—are meant to help you strengthen the Anwei, from which (or whom) you have inherited everything. It is important to strengthen the Anwei because while they can live indefinitely, they are not immune to death. Entire species go extinct with shocking regularity. While every lineage has its relative strengths and weaknesses, and it is difficult if not impossible to judge one as "superior" or "inferior" to another due to the differences in values between them, the standard of survival is universal. The dodo bird and the crow may each have their merits, but the former no longer exists. Whether or not it was better or worse than the crow is irrelevant. One could argue that in terms of beauty, their loss was not a great one, relative to the Tasmanian tiger or the auroch, but no matter how one judges the aesthetic merits or shortcomings of a population, its survival is a necessary precondition.

Suppose that after careful consideration, you conclude that our Anwei is more closely on the trajectory of the dodo bird than the crow. This could mean that you worry about your children being able to work a decent job, or that in two hundred years time, your descendants won't exist. Understanding the concept of the Anwei can help diagnose the source of the danger, and respond to the threat or adapt to the change appropriately. If you are concerned that our identity faces a serious health risk, then you can devote your time to the study of the human body and how to be healthy. You can teach your children the habits of good health, and encourage them to marry healthy partners. If you are concerned about political threats, you could relocate to a safer area (bearing in mind the costs discussed earlier), or persuade other members of your nation to pay attention to these threats and to take appropriate precautions. If you are concerned about the standing and perceived importance of our Anwei, you might dedicate your time and effort to its body of artistic or literary work, or become an engineer or inventor.

Men are generally expected to take an active role in all of these endeavors, and will be looked down upon if they do not. Women can be active in these roles as well, but are usually not looked down upon as failures if they do not, because—as previously discussed—making children is a critically important role which women alone can perform. But women can passively serve the interests of the Anwei doubly by choosing to marry men who strengthen the identity, or who have the qualities that are likely to result in its improvement. Not only does this create children, but it creates an incentive for men to act in ways that are good for the Anwei, rather then in parasitic fashions that are good for themselves at the expense of the group. And to the degree that these positive qualities may be genetic, it replicates what is best, what is strongest, what is most noble, and what is most beautiful within the Anwei.

I myself am blessed to have not only a gorgeous wife whose intelligence hones my own like iron on iron, but who holds me to a standard of excellence so that I might be a source of reassurance to her parents and pride to my own. And of course, there are the children: as I look at my daughter's face while writing this, I am gripped by the hopeful, fearful excitement that she might grow up to be sharper and wiser than myself.

VII. Individualism with a Home

After all of this criticism of individualism, it may sound inconsistent of me to talk of avatars of the Anwei becoming individuals. But that is what this has been about all along: how do you become the best version of yourself? In the final analysis, the collectivism implicit in this understanding of the Anwei and the individualism implied in talk about "self-actualization" are not opposed to each other. Accepting that you are a part of a greater whole is not a danger to your individuality, but the first step in becoming a truly authentic individual.

One of my favorite songs touches on the reason why:

> *You, who are on the road*
> *Must have a code that you can live by.*
> *And so become yourself*
> *Because the past is just a good bye*[34]

In order to become anything at all, you must commit to an exclusive standard that may expose you to judgment, positive or negative. The problem with individualism as many young people pursue it is not that they wish to be individuals, but that they wish to free themselves from the judgmental eye. But that path leads to no accomplishments or legacies, nothing to be proud of. And it fails anyways: you can be judged by how completely you have freed yourself from the tethers of the opinion of others.

---

[34] Nash, Graham. "Teach Your Children." *Déjà Vu.* Atlantic Records, 11 Mar, `1970.

We all must choose a standard against which we can be judged, and by which we can improve as individuals. The only question, then, is what is the best standard? And who are the best judges?

The Anwei is the entity that is invested in you. It is the only being, in fact, whose fate is tied to yours, and who cares for you as itself. Your family, your tribe, and your nation—living or not—are the source and the essence of the code that can allow you to become an individual, and are the people to whom your individuality *matters*. For this reason, aligning yourself with the Anwei is the path to becoming your true self and your best self. It is the way to authentic and real individuality.

The problem with the "individualism" of today is not that it aims towards making you an individual, but that it fails to deliver its promise. By separating us from our Anwei—really, from ourselves—modern individualism makes us into anxious and credulous drifters, buoys without anchors floating on a sea of shifting tides and wayward currents. This does not cut us from our deep need to belong, however, and we are likely to desperately attach ourselves to all manner of other identities: cults, fringe political or religious movements, hobby clubs, or any number of other social organizations seeking to fill the void left in our hearts where connection to the Anwei belongs. Individualism does not *succeed* in making us individuals, free from the oppressive constraints of culture. It only cuts us from the most meaningful ties, whose constraining tendencies are not oppressive in nature, but are the best means of forming us into our best selves.

If you were playing an instrument like the violin, is true freedom achieved by running from the constraints imposed by the nature of the instrument itself? Or is it achieved by submitting yourself to the constraints of the instrument's nature, and through this submission, learning to master it?

I'm sure you can intuit that true freedom and the joys of competence are achieved by the latter path, not the former. But the same is true of yourself; only by accepting what you are and submitting your desires to your own inner nature can you begin to become your own master. This is what Socrates meant when he admonished the aspiring philosopher to *know thyself.*

You are a part and manifestation of the greater whole. Living in alignment with this greater whole is not a threat to your freedom and individuality, but the best—the *only*—path to these, and to a higher, transcendent meaning that is neither delusional nor self-defeating.

I am not contradicting myself: sometimes, living for the Anwei means making decisions that run contrary to the desires, thoughts, and traditions of your ancestors and family. As I already told you, it is very easy for us to get left behind by the world. It is easy for us to see this in our grandparents, and sometimes in our parents too. You should always trust your family over society when this conflict is generated by the culture, because the interests and motivations of the culture-shapers are difficult to identify and are rarely as benign and selfless as they appear. However, it is still sometimes true that our elders can be lost to mercurial world. It is your obligation to the Anwei that you act as an individual, rather than as a mindless slave to the desires of your family and your community. It is also your obligation to your elders and to yourself that you refrain from bitterness, condescension, or contempt towards those left behind in this way. You too will one day be left behind by the world, as they appear to be.

If you have lived as a legacy to the Anwei, you will survive long after your body dies.

§

But what if the Anwei itself dies? What if the legacy you have built collapses into the graveyard of history, like nearly all the other lineages and species the world has hosted?

This is a question that requires addressing because it appears both statistically and logically likely. The eventual death of our sun, the likelihood of nuclear war, the social and psychological threats of technological dependency, and many other dangers lurk in the future for our line, and make death all but inevitable. It is this concern, I suspect, which inclines some towards the worship of a Christian God, or some other deity defined outside of the real world of space and time. But Gods too can die, even if God is "the creative force in the universe" or some other generic and ambiguous concept. Why should this not one day cease?

I do not know what comes after the death of the lineage. Perhaps nothing comes afterwards. But I urge you not to abandon the Anwei, because nothing I have said so far is threatened by the eventuality of total death.

We are still human beings, still socially connected and driven by some things more than others, still capable of laughter and tears, fear and courage, love and hatred, and awe. We have all the time until that death to live as best we can, and the importance of this life that we have together is made emphatic, not meaningless, by its impermanence. It makes living together as we were designed, and not as isolated wanderers, all the more important. All of the thoughts of the existentialists, of the importance of *now*, and of the timelessness that can be captured in a single moment, all of these principles apply to the Anwei in exactly the same way that they apply to an individual. The entire history of a lineage may hinge on the decision of a single person, and every other member of that lineage is a part of that decision. They are the creators of, and beneficiaries of, that single person. They share in that one person's fate. They are the same Anwei.

Just as you and I are the same Anwei.

Earlier I told you that I hoped that my daughter would be smarter and wiser than myself. This is a sentiment I learned to value from a martial arts teacher I once had, whose aim was to train students to be better than himself. This idea goes back even further in history to Homer's *Iliad*, where Hector looks at his son Astyanax and says:

> *Zeus and ye other gods, grant that this my child may likewise prove, even as I, pre-eminent amid the Trojans, as valiant in might, and that he rule mightily over Ilios. And some day may some men say of him as he cometh back from war, 'He is better far than his father.'*

The tragic conclusion of this Homeric story, however, is that after Hector is killed and Troy is conquered, Astyanax was hurled to his death from the city walls. Hector's wish never came true. Yet the power of his motivation still compelled him to live a noble and glorious life, which we still read about 4,000 years later.

This brings me to an ironic conclusion of a circle. You are not exactly an individual, and yet "individualism" within the context of the Anwei is not merely possible, but necessary. But this is individualism with a context—*individualism with a home*. You are not merely yourself, nor do you properly belong to yourself; you were bought with a price[35]. Yet these facts do not diminish our individuality; they *create* it. They give importance to your development as a person and a measure against which your quality *as* an individual may be judged. Your Anwei gives you a heroic mission to embark upon, an object greater than yourself which you were created for, as guardian, caretaker, hero, and savior. Treasure it and guard it with your life, for nothing else matters without it: this is a task for a conscious and sentient individual. Only the best and most diligent might succeed.

Perhaps you have realized now that although I am writing this for you, it is not just for you. I am writing this letter for my parents, grandparents, and ancestors, as a kind of meditation of gratitude. I am writing this for my descendants in general, so that they might benefit from the wisdom I have gained, or might at least be able to find the faults in my wisdom

---

[35] 1 Corinthians 6:19-20

and build upon my mistakes. And I am also writing this to myself, as a reminder of what I believe and a promise to attempt to live in accordance with the principles which I believe to be the highest and most true. But this broadened audience does not diminish the personal nature of this letter, for these other objects are not my target. My goal is to bring honor, glory, and prosperity to the Anwei, and that is a task which the dead and the unborn cannot perform. It is a goal which can only be accomplished by the living, and so it will depend upon you, as an individual.

It is my hope that this letter will be at least half as helpful to you as writing it has been to me. If you take what I say to heart, it is my belief that you will be well on your way to surpassing me in your own relationship with the Anwei, and in living a good life.

In love and sincerity, yours eternal,

—Anwei

Appendix A: What Did the Founders Mean by "Liberty?"[36]

If there is a singular, inarguable principle that lies at the heart of America, it is liberty. The "Statue of Liberty" is perhaps our most iconic landmark, and the "Liberty Bell" in Philadelphia is one of our oldest national symbols. There are more High Schools called "Liberty High School" than seems reasonable. And of course, it is acknowledged in our founding document, which lists securing the "Blessings of Liberty" as the final intended goal of the new government.

But like many words, "liberty" suffers from a plethora of definitions. It can be either an absence of something—i.e., the state of freedom from oppression, restrictions, or rules—or it can be the presence of something—i.e., the possession of "liberties," often in the form of rights. The former is inherently subjective, while the latter is highly contextual, making the use of the word "liberty" a slippery business, particularly when it pertains to law and government.

As perhaps could have been expected, the term has been seized by Libertarians and Liberals, who emphasize that liberty means nothing if not *freedom for the individual*. While intuitive to the modern ear, this understanding is neither the only possible

---

[36] Originally published July, 2018 at *Counter-Currents*. https://www.counter-currents.com/2018/07/what-did-the-founders-mean-by-liberty/

understanding of "liberty," nor is it what the Founding Fathers *meant* by the word.

Consider, by way of explanation, one of the most favored quotes among American Patriots. Benjamin Franklin famously said that "[t]hose who would give up essential Liberty, to purchase a little temporary Safety, deserve neither Liberty nor Safety." This assertion is interpreted as an embodiment of the American attitude which puts liberty (presumably of the individual) above safety (presumably of the collective) in nearly absolute terms.

The only problem is that in context, this famous quote means almost the exact opposite.

The quote comes from a letter written in 1755 by Franklin as a representative of the Pennsylvania Assembly. The letter was addressed to the Governor, whose loyalty seemed torn between the people of Pennsylvania and the proprietary family (the descendants of William Penn), who in fact lived outside of the province but owned a great deal of land there. Recent conflicts with Natives during the French and Indian War required more military supplies and protection along the border regions, which in turn required raising taxes to fund these common defenses. The only problem was that the proposed method of raising these taxes would have taxed the Penn family's lands. This is what is alluded to earlier in the letter when Franklin writes:

Indeed all Bills for raising Money for Publick Use, are so far of the same Kind; but this differs greatly from every former Bill that has been offered him, and all the Amendments (of any Consequence) which he proposed to the Bill he last refused, are in this Bill admitted, save that for totally exempting the Proprietary Estate.

The famous quote itself is preceded by an explanatory statement of the predicament the Pennsylvanians faced what they had done so far to protect themselves, and the limitations they would face in preceding further without the land-taxes they are requesting:

In fine, we have the most sensible Concern for the poor distressed Inhabitants of the Frontiers. We have taken every Step in our Power, consistent with the just Rights of the Freemen of Pennsylvania, for their Relief, and we have Reason to believe, that in the Midst of their Distresses they themselves do not wish us to go farther. Those who would give up essential Liberty, to purchase a little temporary Safety, deserve neither Liberty nor Safety.

"Liberty" in this context refers to the freedom of the citizens to govern themselves and to pass laws as a collective. It is the freedom *of the group*, and not of the individual, which Franklin is appealing to. In fact, it appears that the freedom of the individual—the governor, that is—was the problem, as Benjamin Wittes of Lawfare and the Brookings Institute explains:

What's more the "purchase [of] a little temporary safety" of which Franklin complains was not the ceding of power to a government Leviathan in exchange for some promise of protection from external threat; for in Franklin's letter, the word "purchase" does not appear to have been a metaphor. The governor was accusing the Assembly of stalling on appropriating money for frontier defense by insisting on including the Penn lands in its taxes–and thus triggering his intervention. And the Penn family later offered cash to fund defense of the frontier–as long as the Assembly would acknowledge that it lacked the power to tax the family's lands. Franklin was thus complaining of the choice facing the legislature between being able to make funds available for frontier defense and maintaining its right of self-governance–and he was criticizing the governor for suggesting it should be willing to give up the latter to ensure the former.

To summarize, the Pennsylvanians sought the "liberty" of self-governance through raising taxes on everyone via the provincial government. This conflicted with the "safety" of the proprietary family and the provincial governor representing the proprietary family's interests.

Of course, we can reach this conclusion about intended meaning of "liberty" through the Declaration of Independence itself, which cites as its very first complaints how the King of England has "refused his assent to laws, the most wholesome and necessary for the public good," and has variously prevented the Colonists from being able to govern themselves. It would not be overstating things to say that the colonists were not complaining about an *excess* of government so much as they were complaining of a *lack* of effective government. This absence of government, not its oppressive presence, was the impediment to liberty and prosperity which our Founding Father fought a war to do away with.

The Founding Fathers were not libertarian individualists. We know this from the fasces they adorned their buildings with, and we know this from their acknowledgment of differences between groups—something which leftists hold as evidence of racism at the very beginning of American history, but which also applies to distinctions *between* white groups. Benjamin Franklin himself, incidentally, held reservations about the Germans in particular:

Why should Pennsylvania, founded by the English, become a Colony of Aliens, who will shortly be so numerous as to Germanize us instead of our Anglifying them, and will never adopt our Language or Customs, any more than they can acquire our Complexion.

But most importantly, we know this from their statements about Liberty in our founding documents. Loving liberty does not require one to be an individualist, as an American or in general. To the contrary, the Founding Fathers understood that organizing around the collective interests of the group, rather than those of the individual, is the best way to achieve the most liberty.

APPENDIX B: CURSED ARE THE PEACE-ENFORCERS[37]

Blessed are the peacemakers: for they shall be called the children of God.
–Matthew 5:9

Everyone looks up to the work of "peace-making," whether it is for secular humanitarian justifications or for religious ones. No one wants to be the source of conflict, yet many go above and beyond this general standard, seeking not only to avoid starting disputes, but to *make peace*. But what does it mean to "make peace?" The question is less obvious than it at first appears, because in different senses of the phrase, the spirit beneath the word may be contradictory.

Consider the story of Adam and Bob. The two brothers get into a dispute. For the sake of simplicity, let us assume that the brothers are five, and the dispute is over a toy. There are two directions this dispute could take. First, the two brothers could work towards a resolution between themselves. Second, the mother could intervene and resolve the dispute for them.

On the first path, it is possible that the dispute escalates to the point that one boy kills the other. This is wildly unlikely, which means that a dispute

---

[37] Originally published Jan, 2018 at *Caffeine & Philosophy*. https://caffeineandphilosophy.com/2018/01/02/cursed-are-the-peace-enforcers/

which is not resolved to both boys' satisfaction will likely reemerge at a later date. Each brother will have to learn to get along with the other if he wants to avoid being miserable himself. This is how children gradually acquire the skills of empathy and the foundational instincts of game-theory-morality. Conflict, in other words, generates the environment necessary to learn the skills that will be expected of us as mature adults.

What of the second path? What if the mother intervenes and "makes peace" between her two sons, perhaps distracting and placating them, or maybe even adjudicating the dispute in one side's favor? Trying to get their minds off the matter will certainly solve the immediate predicament, but it does so at the cost of the experience the children would gain in learning to make peace among themselves.

This pattern emerges in parental modeling as well. Recent psychological research seems to indicate that conflicts between parents in can actually be *beneficial* to the children, so long as the resolution to the argument is also observed:

> Some types of conflicts are not disturbing to kids, and kids actually benefit from it," says Cummings [E. Mark Cummings, Notre Dame University]. When parents have mild to moderate conflict that involves support and compromise and positive emotions, children develop better social skills and self-esteem, enjoy increased emotional security, develop better relationships with parents, do better in school and have fewer psychological problems.

"When kids witness a fight and see the parents resolving it, they're actually happier than they were before they saw it," says Cummings. "It reassures kids that parents can work things through. We know this by the feelings they show, what they say, and their behavior—they run off and play. Constructive conflict is associated with better outcomes over time."

Even if parents don't completely resolve the problem but find a partial solution, kids will do fine. "Compromise is best, but we have a whole lot of studies that show that kids benefit from any progress toward resolution," says Cummings.

By contrast, children who witness even a moderate argument, but who are not allowed to witness the resolution, experience a gradual building of tension and stress around the relationship. Resolution to arguments proves that relationships with people are resilient, even antifragile. Unresolved arguments, by contrast, tend to inflame and enlarge the tension and anxiety surrounding relationships. The world becomes unstable when there is no clear pattern linking calm to storm-clouds, and no visible path from the latter back to the former.

This means that the mother of Adam and Bob, in her intervention, is actually *robbing her sons of the experience necessary to become peacemakers themselves.*

This simple and illustrative example is by no means a catch-all, implying that in no circumstances should a parent ever intercede in their children's interactions. Rather, it is a criticism of a particular reason *why* parents–or friends, family, even strangers–may intercede in a nearby conflict: "conflict is bad, so I will stop the conflict, and this will make me good." Or, "conflict is bad because I cannot tolerate it, so I will stop it."

In my recent debate with Zach Ryan Mora on Satanism, I argued that the essential quality of what is satanic is that which is proud and what is judgmental and accusatory in its pride. It may sound a little hyperbolic to describe self-appointed peace-enforcers, who come around and battle against conflict on other's behalf, as "satanic," but it touches on a real pulse.

Whether they are unable to cope with the potential instability they associate with conflict, or they can't resist the impulse to push others down to elevate themselves, those who make peace *or else* are not doing God's work. This is why Dolores Umbridge is such an easy character to hate: under the pretense of being nice, she neither wanted nor tolerated disagreement, and stifled everything that was good in the process.

Intolerance for disagreement is stifling and hateful because what is good, what is beautiful, what is noble, what is pure, and what is true, all matter. Being able to distinguish these qualities from their opposites are what makes life itself either good or bad, and since no one person has the answers, or will *ever* have all the answers, the sincere pursuit of the good within life will inevitably lead to disagreement, perhaps even conflict. But this conflict is not antithetical to what is *good*; it is only antithetical to peace.

Arguments and debate represent turning points in the recursive oscillations that move us closer and closer to the ideals that make life good. The helicopter moms and Dolores Umbridges of the world impede, or even obstruct, these oscillations, perhaps out of pride or fear, maybe even envy. But this behavior is not "peacemaking," in the sense intended in the beattitudes. A more complete elaboration on what "peacemaking" looks like can be found later on in the book of Matthew:

> Moreover if thy brother shall trespass against thee, go and tell him his fault between thee and him alone: if he shall hear thee, thou hast gained thy brother.
> But if he will not hear thee, then take with thee one or two more, that in the mouth of two or three witnesses every word may be established. And if he shall neglect to hear them, tell it unto the church: but if he neglect to hear the church, let him be unto thee as an heathen man and a publican[38].

Biblical peacemaking does not avoid confrontation, but actually *requires* it. It is also not pursued on another's behalf, but on one's own behalf: first because we all have our own troubles that are likely great enough; second, because we may not be aware of the full extent of the subject; third, allowing people to become outraged on other's behalf opens the door to all sorts of perverse incentives and social power-plays, and there is no end to that hallway.

---

[38] Tax-collector.

In other words, what Jesus advocates is not "peace" per se when he says "blessed are the peacemakers."

> *Think not that I am come to send peace on earth: I came not to send peace, but a sword.*
> *–Matthew 10:34*

Rather, what he advocates is *reconciliation*. Reconciliation is itself a form of forgiveness, which is arguably the heart of Christian spiritual practice: "...forgive us our sins, as we forgive those who sin against us."

No one is perfect, which means that participation in the dance means we will inevitably miss some steps. There are two options: correction (and forgiveness), or stepping out. There is no way to take option one and also have peace: the only peace that is even *theoretically* possible is the silence of death. Whether that death is literal or figurative is essentially irrelevant for those who live there. Life is conflict. There's simply no getting around it, and it's a living death to move about the world avoiding any and all collisions with other people.

So blessed are the peacemakers, for they keep fighting fun, and life vivacious. And cursed are the peace-enforcers, who condemn life itself as intolerable or immoral, even if they themselves do not know it.

Appendix C: Identity and the Problem with Christianity[39]

Whenever we accept certain axioms as true, we bar ourselves from accepting certain conclusions which contradict the axioms. For example, if we accept the axioms that identity matters, and that race is a component of identity, then one cannot claim that race does not matter.

Identity is valuable because it gives coherence to our relationships with our ancestors and descendants, it builds social trust and solidarity in our communities, and it helps establish who we are as individuals. Without such an understanding or awareness of who we are, any greater purpose or justification for life can be difficult to ascertain. Race is a large component of identity that has been neglected in recent decades, so naturally, identitarians ought to care about race.

But race is not the only component of identity. Indeed, in many circumstances and situations, it may not even be the most critical component of identity. Religion often competes with race for predominance, and the axioms of identity and the barring of certain conclusions apply to religion in the same manner that they apply to race.

What I am about to say may seem divisive in an already weak movement, and as such, inappropriate

---

[39] Originally published June, 2018 at *Counter-Currents*. https://www.counter-currents.com/2018/06/identity-and-the-problem-with-christianity/

as a subject. But there is an old tale about the importance of building one's house upon solid rock, rather than on sand, because no matter how well-built the house may be, a weak foundation will bring it all crashing down when the winds begin to blow. Religion being a critical component to the foundations of identity, it should be taken seriously because smaller differences than religion have fractured nations when allowed to fester.

First let me give a little bit of relevant personal background. I have spent the last two and a half years attempting, to the best of my ability, to be a Christian. I grew up Christian and was reasonably well-read. Like many teenagers, I was heavily influenced by the New Atheists, particularly Christopher Hitchens and Richard Dawkins, and left the faith in my sophomore year of High School, gradually maturing into the most insufferable variety of atheist.

After discovering Joseph Campbell several years later, my tune began to change. Maybe I had been thinking about religion all wrong this whole time?

My first inclination, incidentally, was not Christianity but paganism. I had been learning and adapting myself more and more to pagan beliefs, until it occurred to me that within both Christian *and* Pagan worldviews, social relationships are not merely important, but are in many ways the heart of spirituality. My family was Christian; my wife was Christian; my in-laws were culturally Christian; my extended family were all Christian or culturally Christian. Wouldn't it be a selfish abandonment of my family to become pagan? Wouldn't it be arrogant of me to assume that I knew something they did not, and to separate myself religiously from them?

And so I adopted Christianity: for my family, informed by mythological parable, and grounded in faith. This to me seemed like an adequate justification to choose Christianity, or to seriously choose any other religion for that matter.

As it turns out, this line of reasoning is compatible with paganism, but is incompatible with Christianity:

> Now therefore fear the Lord, and serve him in sincerity and in truth: and put away the gods which your fathers served on the other side of the flood, and in Egypt; and serve ye the Lord.

> And if it seem evil unto you to serve the Lord, choose you this day whom ye will serve; whether the gods which your fathers served that were on the other side of the flood, or the gods of the Amorites, in whose land ye dwell: but as for me and my house, we will serve the Lord.
> —Joshua 24:14-15

In the Old Testament, and the New:

> If any man come to me, and hate not his father, and mother, and wife, and children, and brethren, and sisters, yea, and his own life also, he cannot be my disciple.
> —Luke 14:26

Holding to Christianity because it is the religion of your fathers is, according to scripture, the incorrect reason.

Needless to say, I had a hard time with the literal truth of the doctrine, but what of the metaphorical value? What if Adam was an archetypal representation of the evil in man that we all recognized, and Christ's redemption of man was, in his humanity, an act so good—and through it, proof that man was *capable* of such an act—that by itself, his death on the cross gave us reason to hope in others, here on this earth? And isn't the Kingdom of God within us?

As with the religion of the father, this logic actually does apply to paganism, but fails with Christianity, no matter what Campbell or his modern avatar, Jordan Peterson, might say. Even Bishop Robert Barron, who presents a great defense of the classical conception of God more sophisticated than what the New Atheists generally attack, has a critical word to say about their gnostisizing tendency, to "bracket historicity, to uncover a sort of secret or hidden wisdom in these texts." The danger, according to Barron, is missing the immense importance of *whether or not certain things happened*. Ultimately, Christianity does not, and cannot, boil down to psycho-narrative interpretations of world forces. It hinges upon Jesus, the person, actually dying on an actual cross, and actually, literally, rising from the dead three days later. If this did not happen, or if we are not given the chance of immortality as a result of its happening, then according to the Church fathers themselves, Christianity is *wrong*.

> *And if Christ be not risen, then is our preaching vain, and your faith is also vain.*
> —1 Corinthians 15:14

What about faith?

Faith is the last, and the strongest justification. Casually dismissed as "wishful thinking" by Hitchens, it is the great Kierkegaardian leap that allows us to act even in the face of uncertainty. But what should we have faith in? The case for Christian faith lies, to a great degree, in the attractiveness of its story and its metaphysical conception of the universe. The reason to have faith in Christianity—as opposed to faith in another religion—is because the story is comforting, encouraging, and life-giving. All "informed by reason" too, of course.

Here is where the conflict between Christianity and identitarianism comes becomes important.

First of all, I don't mean identitarianism in the petty, political sense. Politics is always a means to an end, and if politics were conflicting with spiritual matters, it is obvious we ought to choose the latter. But identity itself is a spiritual matter, and the conflict cuts to the heart of what it means to be an individual in the modern world.

First, Christians accept that all people are "image-bearers" of God, and are intrinsically worthy of respect as not only creations of God, but in many ways as proxies for God himself:

And the King shall answer and say unto them, Verily I say unto you, Inasmuch as ye have done it unto one of the least of these my brethren, ye have done it unto me.

Then shall he say also unto them on the left hand, Depart from me, ye cursed, into everlasting fire, prepared for the devil and his angels:

> *For I was an hungred, and ye gave me no meat: I was thirsty, and ye gave me no drink:*
>
> *I was a stranger, and ye took me not in: naked, and ye clothed me not: sick, and in prison, and ye visited me not.*
>
> *Then shall they also answer him, saying, Lord, when saw we thee an hungred, or athirst, or a stranger, or naked, or sick, or in prison, and did not minister unto thee?*
>
> *Then shall he answer them, saying, Verily I say unto you, Inasmuch as ye did it not to one of the least of these, ye did it not to me.*
> —*Matthew 25:40-45*

Christianity in this way holds us to be our brother's keeper. But our brother is not merely our biological brother; in Christ, all believers are family, are one:

> *There is neither Jew nor Greek, there is neither bond nor free, there is neither male nor female: for ye are all one in Christ Jesus.*
> —*Galatians 3:28*

This famous Galatians verse does not, incidentally, deny basic national and biological differences between people, but rather establishes an ethical obligation between the body of believers that is familial. This familial bond is often even extended to *unbelievers* by particularly zealous Christians, who trust the welfare of their families, their nations, and themselves to foreigners and strangers who do not share their faith. This is not theologically sound, so far as I can tell, but it is illustrative in its visible instincts of how Christians are expected to treat other Christians. Those who have faith in Christ are brothers in Christ.

This creates a number of problems relating to identity.

First, our identities as individuals are not revealed by removing or blurring connections with others but are forged *through* connection with others. These other people cannot be just anybody, as the first set of connections is one that we are born into: namely, the genetic connection with our parents and our ancestors. Biological brothers and sisters fall within this familial category as well. They are our *real* family. Christianity, by first requiring us to leave our family in order to follow Christ, and second by expanding our "family" to extraordinary, inhuman proportions, diminishes our ability to establish a coherent self that is reliable to others, because it denies the inherent validity and importance of the core relationships that ground us and shape us into beings that can connect with our parents. The only route of authentic reconnection for the parent to the Christian child is through Christianity; the fact that these parents created you and raised you from infancy is not sufficient, because we are told that our parents did not *really* create you. God did that.

It should be said that there *is* a real intimacy in Christian relationships, which I do not mean to dismiss. But it is a distinct and separate kind of relationship, one which is shoulder-to-shoulder, rather than face-to-face. Both parties face together towards God, and learn about each other by learning about God, to the degree that each continues in their faith and emulation of Jesus.

But God is not merely the object of attention. He is also the eternal observer and the final adjudicator. We are never completely alone with someone else, nor, in the final analysis, does God permit the resolution of disputes between individuals to be handled by these individuals. While Matthew 18:15-17 pays lip-service to the procedure of resolving disputes amongst individuals, it is only lip-service because within the Christian framework, it is not other people whom we wrong, but God. The fact is that other people are, as people, only proxies for God, deserving of respect precisely—and *solely*—because they are image-bearers of God (God being the only proper object of worship). When we wrong other people, the victim is not the actual person wronged, but God. Even if the Christian acknowledges that there is something intrinsically wrong with harming another person regardless of God (many of their moral arguments hinge upon this point being false), the wrong against the individual is so petty, in scope, in injustice, and in consequences, compared to the wrong done to God that it is *relatively* meaningless.

Human relationships aren't fundamentally built upon getting along with each other. That's a necessary condition, most of the time, but if you simply agree with someone on absolutely everything, you will not develop the deepest kinds of human bonds. Those are acquired through having and resolving conflicts. By relocating the conflict from between two individuals and making it between the individual and God, we deny ourselves the opportunity to develop deep relationships with others and are redirected instead to deepening our relationship with God.

This redirection threatens intimacy—at least the face-to-face variety—but it also threatens the classical notion of honor, which requires us to stick up for ourselves and to care about our reputation. Within the Christian worldview, vengeance belongs to the Lord. It is God's task—not yours—to take care of yourself and your reputation.

All of this culminates in a kind of spirituality that is rightly credited as the antecedent to modern conceptions of individualism, wherein human identity is *truly* discovered by removing ourselves from all ties to the earth, rather than identifying what those ties are and refining them.

The modern world presents us with a serious problem. The unholy scale of human migration we are experiencing has not been seen ever before in human history. Historically, genocides, the collapses of empires, the forging of new peoples and the destruction of old nations usually followed such movements, and survival in such turbulent seas requires a heavy anchor and a strong rope. It requires a clear sense of identity, so that when that identity comes under attack, the attack can be identified and defended against.

What does Christianity have to say about this? It requires one to be at worst, ambivalent. Life on this earth is ultimately of no importance, after all. On the other hand, many view the movement and migration as a *good* thing. Why? Not merely from fear and trepidation around open-borders progressives. Just last week, I was at an evangelism conference, and the speaker was saying how wonderful it was that all of these refugees were coming in because we could all proselytize to unbelievers without having to cross an ocean. They were coming to us! How wonderful!

Even caring about the demographic dangers, let alone bringing them up, violated Galatians 3:28. Don't you know that these immigrants are your brothers too? And don't you know that you are your brother's keeper?

Within Christianity, there is neither mother nor father, daughter nor son, stranger nor friend; for all are one in Christ. There is no cohesive identity in Christianity, no identifiable self or lineage to get upset about should it be put in danger of annihilation. The Lord giveth, and the Lord taketh away. The indifference to life, to family, and to nation (relative to God) that Christianity requires makes it a path of death in the modern age.

I understand that the historically-minded Christians may point back to a history of great civilization under Christendom and ask how these conclusions could possibly be justified in the face of the facts. Indeed, the West *has* achieved great things under the Christian flag, but the attribution of this success to Christianity is not merely questionable, but theologically unsound, placing value on worldly accomplishments rather than upon godliness of the spirit. This was a point which Augustine makes in *City of God*, when confronting Pagans who blamed the rise of Christianity for the collapse and sacking of Rome:

> *If those who lost their earthly riches in that disaster had possessed them in the spirit thus described to them by one who was outwardly poor but inwardly rich; that is, if they had 'used the*

world as though not using it,' then they would have been able to say, with that man who was so sorely tried and yet was never overcome: 'I issued from my mother's womb in nakedness, and in nakedness I shall return to the Earth. The Lord has given, the Lord has taken away. It has happened as God decided. May the Lord's name be blessed.' Thus a good servant would regard the will of God as his great resource, and he would be enriched in his mind by close attendance on God's will; nor would he grieve if deprived in life of those possessions which he would soon have to leave behind at his death.

—*Augustine of Hippo,* City of God

Even if most believers don't understand or accept the true ferocity of this dedication, their allegiance to the faith will eventually leave them morally powerless to oppose those who *do* sincerely adopt the principles of Christian identity unadorned with un-Christian idols, like "survival." I think we are reaching this point of conflict, which does not require us to run like cowards from our spiritual loyalties, but rather *reveals* that the Christian God is not in fact the God of the living, but the God of the dead and soon-to-be dead.

The astute Christian reader will recognize that this whole argument has no power whatsoever if the religion is, in fact, true. But for those who are uncertain or uninterested in the truth, but are coming to the realization that spirituality matters, and consider Christianity to be a viable candidate for their own mytho-poetic spiritual exploration, you should understand that Christianity is incompatible with any form of identity other than that of being a Christian. The Christian God is a jealous God, and there is no room for serving multiple masters. There is but one God, and nothing—*nothing*—else matters.

Made in the USA
San Bernardino, CA
17 November 2018